Marketing Magic
for
Volunteer Programs

by

Sue Vineyard

Foreword by Marlene Wilson

Published by
Heritage Arts Publishing
1807 Prairie Avenue
Downers Grove, Illinois 60515
(312) 964-1194

To my parents, Kay and Ralph Wylie,
who without knowing it, taught me
marketing by teaching me about
the value of caring relationships.

ACKNOWLEDGMENTS

The writing of any book can never be a singular effort. Many people play a vital role in its creation, either from the standpoint of its physical production or through the critically important aspect of support of the writer. Several such people have helped this work go from dream to reality, and I am deeply indebted to each of them.

Marlene Wilson, who encouraged me from the dream stage on, read every word of my first draft, offering suggestions and comments, in addition to her Foreword, that I know made the book much the richer and more meaningful. As ever, I owe a great deal to her wisdom, patience and loving concern.

Betty Mitchell is the poor soul who had to take all my pages of hand-written thoughts and with the aid of her trusty Apple computer make them come out so others could read them. She also oversaw the actual production of the book, making sure page 42 was in at least close proximity to pages 41 and 43!

Nora M. Holmes was the wizzard that then took those pages and typeset them beautifully. Finding Nora was a gift from the good Lord, who obviously looks out for authors with little knowledge of the world of pica, Helvetica and hanging indents!

At this point Chris Winter of the Reporter/Progress Publications here in Downers Grove stepped in to print the final copy, turning Nora and Betty's work into the product you are now reading.

Support also came in the form of patience from my husband Wes and sons Bill and Bob, who put up with piles of books, copy and artwork all over our home and many fast food meals when Mom was "on a roll." Even Meghan, our black lab seemed to know when to keep out of my way and not ask to be let out!

And lastly to a group of people who simply by their faith in me offered support and encouragement . . . Laura Lee Geraghty, Chris Franklin, Betty Greer, Ed and Louise Mitchell, Ivan Scheier, Karlene and Dick Krajewski. Thank you all for being there.

Table of Contents

FOREWORD

Now that volunteer administration has come of age as a field, it is vital that we continue to expand our skills and knowledge. We must always value the strength that comes from competency.

It is for just that reason that this book by Sue Vineyard is of great importance to volunteer directors and leaders. It deals with a discipline that is little understood and therefore poorly utilized by far too many people in human services. We believe in our causes passionately, but often have great difficulty in marketing those causes to others.

Since needs almost always outstrip resources, we constantly must seek out volunteers, money, support and facilities . . . and yet we are often uneasy, reluctant and almost embarrassed to ask for what we need.

Sue addresses the problem in clear, specific and no-nonsense language that helps the novice not only understand marketing, but more importantly, to be able to do it. She even manages to make it exciting and fun!

Sue Vineyard writes from a rich background of experience both as a fund raiser and manager of volunteers. As always, advice from someone who has "been in the trenches" somehow seems to work so much better than that coming from someone who simply addresses a topic academically or philosophically. This book is meant to be used as a work book and has been written by someone who has made it work.

I believe it will become a valuable resource for all those who have learned the hard way that wishing will not make it so. Planning, determination and skill are what sell people on ideas and causes as well as products. *Marketing Magic for Volunteer Programs* provides all three.

Marlene Wilson
September, 1984

Marketing Magic
For Volunteer Programs

*"We shall not cease from exploration and the
end of all our exploring will be to arrive where we
started and know the place for the first time."*
T. S. Eliot

MARKETING . . . by my count that word consists of nine letters from the English alphabet, yet as I travel extensively, training for non-profit groups, I find that many people are convinced it's a four-letter word written in some mystical language.

Let's take the mystery out of marketing while at the same time letting its magic shine through!

Marketing has really been around since time began. . . . but it's been going by other names, such as:

> sharing
> trading
> exchanging
> bartering, etc.

Although I can't prove it, I have a strong hunch "marketing" first appeared when Eve said, "Hey Adam, if you'll just reach me a few of those forbidden apples I'll cook you a strudel you won't forget!" Well, maybe that's not the best example, but you get my drift.

Marketing marched on through the ages, for the most part enjoying a good reputation (KING ARTHUR: "If you will sit at my round table and help make the decisions, we'll all share in the riches of the land." COLUMBUS: "Queenie, you give me three ships and I'll go discover America for you." Enterprising Architect: "Tut, if you let me design your tomb I guarantee nobody will find it and mess it up until the nose of the sphinx wears off.")

Unfortunately, marketing got a bad name a couple of hundred years ago in America when some slick city dudes said, "Tell you what chief, we'll trade you this pile of genuine, sparkle-plenty beads for that crummy old island off New York. Whaddayasay, buddy?"

From that point on it became a real chore to convince people that marketing was not some kind of con-game, where the asker (the marketer) tries to slip something over on the unsuspecting consumer by using hard-sell tactics, guilt-trips, "shoulds and oughts," and assorted threats against favorite pets and relatives in Peoria.

Sadly, this misconception seems to have taken root most deeply in people involved in human service groups. If you don't believe this to be true, stop the most conservative and devoted member of your board of directors and suggest that your organization consider switching to a total marketing orientation. You can expect a reply that begins with a sniff and goes on to state, "We simply don't believe in such tactics."

As we approach the end of the 20th century and look toward the 21st, we, in the growing human service business, must not only erase the incredibly negative misconceptions about marketing but also learn to master its positive lessons in order that we offer a fair value return to clients, volunteers, and donors in exchange for their involvement in our causes.

Let's start with a definition of marketing in terms we, in human services, can appreciate:

MARKETING IS THE CARING TRADE OF VALUE FOR VALUE

This means that when our organization identifies a need it has for volunteers, it figures out what value it might offer those volunteers in exchange for their efforts.

An example might be the need for a volunteer to design and paint six posters for use in the hospital gift shop. In exchange for this work the hospital volunteer department could offer:

1. Recognition in the volunteer newsletter for the artist.
2. Documentation of the work for a future resume.
3. Satisfaction of helping.
4. Joy of being able to display a talent.
5. Skill building.
6. A letter of appreciation for the artist sent to employer, church, family, etc.

The true "magic" of marketing comes when all parties involved in an exchange relationship are convinced they have received the greatest value.

Throughout this book I will share with you the application of marketing principles to the voluntary sector—and more specifically, the Volunteer Department and leadership of non-profit groups—first by laying down the principles, then through examples and check lists, providing step by step "how to" suggestions. For those of you who like your learning stripped to the bone, the last chapter provides a recipe for marketing applied to the attainment of volunteers, supporters, and donors.

After all that, it's up to you—even though this book has the word "magic" in its title, it does NOT come equipped with a magic wand!

Like any of the tools needed to manage a well-run program, it takes lots of hard work, creative problem-solving, and innovative thinking to make it happen!

I know you can do it!

CHAPTER I

A Few Basics
Before You Begin

"The greatest revolution in our generation
is that human beings, by changing the inner attitudes
of their minds can change the outer aspects of their lives."
. . . William James

"Denial is the alternative to transformation."
. . . Alice Sargent[7]

THE MARKETING CONCEPT

Adam and Eve, King Tut, and Columbus not withstanding—let's look at where literature first began talking about a "marketing concept" and understand how it came about.

First formulated in the 1950's for business firms, the marketing concept was an alternative to two previous methods of doing business.[1]

These two methods were:

Production Orientation: This focused on providing products needed by people. There was little need for research or advertising as this orientation came about when people's incomes were low and needs centered on basics of clothing, food, and shelter (the base of Maslow's Hierarchy of Needs reviewed in Chapter 4). There was little guesswork in knowing what people desired nor much concern about customer satisfaction because there were so many customers waiting for goods. The products were kept simple, and energies went toward increasing output and reducing costs. (Sometimes at the expense of product quality.) There was an attitude that people would never stop needing their products. Many companies of this era made only one product, such as cloth diapers, tooth powder, dry starch, spats, and cranks for Model T's.

Sales Orientation: When the economy grew more affluent and buyers had satisfied their basic needs, they had the extra resources to spend by choice. This caused businesses to try to attract buyers, convincing them they wanted—even needed—their products. The customer was enticed into buying through promotion that often played on emotional and status appeals. The main purpose of the business was to create high demands for their products in order to produce high profits. An attitude prevailed that said the customer, once "hooked," would probably come back for more, but if not, there were plenty more customers in the wings.

A NEW LIGHT DAWNS—THE MARKETING ORIENTATION

In the 1950's it dawned on some forward-looking companies that a new set of rules called for a change in philosopohy and orientation to one that favored the consumer as much as it did the producer. It recognized the fact that the customer was more sophisticated and selective and more in tune with various options in addition to his own needs. Thus, the marketing orientation was born.

Companies that saw this new light began to change toward serving a need more than selling a product. They saw their customers as real people, worked to find out their needs, and then created products, services, etc. to *respond* to those needs. More simply put—they designed goods and services that customers wanted.

At that point marketing began to be defined as "the performance of business activities that directs the flow of goods and services from producer to consumer in order to satisfy customers and accomplish the organizations objectives."[2]

THE THREE ORIENTATIONS IN THE VOLUNTARY SECTOR

To understand these three orientations allow me to draw parallels to our voluntary or human service sector, although you may have much better examples from your own experience:

Production Orientation: Many groups exhibit this orientation. They have one product or service (public education, health service, food baskets, counseling for a specific concern), and feel they will always be needed. Effort concentrates on making this service or product more efficient; the agency becomes more and more embroiled in concern for reporting systems, training people to do things "the agency way." Little attention is given to checking with clients or the public to see if, indeed, the "product" is really needed and/or satisfying.

Sales Orientation: It is fairly common for the fundraising department of a charity to get stuck in this mode of thinking. When this is true you usually find that they have one fundraising event (i.e.: a bike-athon, etc.) that they continue to try to promote years after it seems to have lost its appeal to participants. The charity, however, keeps trying to "sell" it as if it were the most exciting thing since sliced bread. They are really just propagandizing their event, however, without really being in tune with public trends that have lead away from their promotion, etc.

Marketing Orientation: Without calling it such, many non-profit groups have embraced this philosophy of identifying real, current needs and adapting programs and services to respond to those needs. Examples include:

1. The YMCA which has adapted programs to meet family needs, stress management, etc.

2. The YWCA which now focuses on career, skill, and personality development of women.

3. Army Community Services which works to involve the total military family in base services, counseling, skill building, etc.

4. Churches which deal with their members wholistically, encouraging the development of skills, gifts, support, etc.

5. Hospitals which, rather than simply being in the business of pills, operations, and rotten food, now see themselves as being in the business of health care, stress management, wellness, disease prevention, education, counseling, support, etc. etc.

THE IMPORTANCE OF MARKETING
FOR VOLUNTEER PROGRAMS

During the summer months, while our son Bob is home from college, he works for a small construction firm that specializes in remodeling.

On his first day he blithly went off to work with his lunch and thermos. Upon his return that evening he said he'd been chastised for not having a hammer of his own, and subsequently proceeded to the hardware store to acquire this basic tool.

That was the first trip of many he eventually made to stores, garage sales, outlets, etc. as he discovered the need for more and more tools to do his work. Each summer the trunk of his car resembles a "going out of business" sale at a carpentry shop, and I have stopped trying to keep all the unusual items straight in my mind, let alone what they are used for.

From this experience Bob has learned a great lesson that will probably serve him well throughout life:

YOU MUST HAVE THE RIGHT TOOLS TO DO A GOOD JOB.

This same lesson holds true for running volunteer programs, managing non-profits, organizing events, etc. etc. . . . You Must Have The Right Tools To Do A Good Job!

FOUR TOOLS FOR SUCCESS

There are four tools that are basic to the success of any volunteer program. Each must be *appreciated,* understood, and mastered. The tools are: MANAGEMENT, MOTIVATION, MARKETING, AND THE ART OF ASKING.

If you wonder why I emphasized the need for *appreciation* of these tools, let me share with you that of these four, two are widely accepted and two are resisted.

THE TWO *ACCEPTED* TOOLS

As you might guess, management and motivation are accepted today as necessary tools, due in great measure to the work of Marlene Wilson, author of the "bible" of the field, *The Effective Management of Volunteer Programs.*[3]

Please know, however, that during the seventies, when Marlene and other leaders such as Ivan Scheier and Harriet Naylor were first introducing management and motivation concepts to the field of volunteerism, they were heavily resisted with the same types of responses that now meet marketing. ("We want to retain the feeling of family." "We don't want to become cold and corporate." "That only works for products!" etc. etc.)

THE TWO *RESISTED* TOOLS

The remaining two tools (marketing and asking) are now being slowly accepted as people become aware of what they are and what they are *not*.

Although we will look at the art of asking in Chapter 5, this work will, primarily, explore the marketing tool thoroughly so that readers may appreciate its value and master its usage.

THE IMPORTANCE OF MARKETING

Let's look at why marketing is so important:

1. *In recruitment:* This is the bridge between potential volunteers and your program. It defines what is needed and what benefits are available in addition to offering incentives to prospective volunteers in order to attract and involve them in your program.

2. *In retention:* The values given volunteers (and paid staff!) in the way of tangible and intangible rewards are what keep volunteers coming back and also stimulates them to tell others about their good feelings, which feeds back in to recruitment.

3. *For organizational climate:* Happy workers who feel good about their work create a climate that stimulates creativity, enjoyment, and achievement. It simply "feels good" to work and be there!

4. *In gaining support:* When, as a director, you need the support of administration, board members, co-workers, peer level department heads, etc., marketing provides the basic leverage that allows you to define an exchange relationship (what's in it for them and you) to attain your goals.

5. *In winning public support:* As you need the support of the general public for your programs, events, philosophies, etc., marketing again holds the key to attaining it. The arm of public relations comes into play in this relationship and is examined in Chapter 6.

6. *In resource development* (fundraising, etc.): When you are in need of goods, services, or dollars, the marketing orientation

is the magic that will produce results. In fact, the use of marketing holds the key to getting what you need *without* spending dollars . . . the art of *friend* raising.

7. *In obtaining clients/members/participants/consumers:* Marketing is again the key in getting people to accept your services and/or products. Its proper application convinces people to become involved with you as they perceive a great value to themselves for that involvement.

Too often, marketing is the missing tool in the volunteer director's tool box, with the result that concerns begin to arise around recruitment, retention, and fundraising. As shrinking resources, higher demands on volunteer's time, and greater client-needs impact us more dramatically each year, we must master this tool in order to achieve the successful attainment of our goals.

THE FUNDAMENTALS OF MARKETING— PUBLICS, MARKETS, AND EXCHANGES

Marketing is made up of three components: PUBLICS, MARKETS, and the EXCHANGE RELATIONSHIP. Let's define all three, as I will refer to them throughout the book.

PUBLIC: any identifiable segment of society that surrounds your program or agency. Publics are groups that you *might* or *might never* want to have a relationship with. When identifying publics you don't worry about or try to judge whether or not you might someday want to interact with them. . . . They simply exist.

Publics can be identified by:

1. Title: Girl Scouts, Lutherans, Red Cross, U.S. Army, etc.

2. Generic quality: married women, school kids, clients, donors, doctors, etc.

3. Classification:

   a. Internal publics: Groups/people who work inside (i.e.: volunteers, paid staff, etc.)

   b. Agent publics: people who speak in behalf of a group, etc. (i.e.: Pastors who refer people to your services, etc.)

   c. Consuming publics: People who use your services (i.e.: clients, consumers, members, general public, etc.]

d. Regulatory publics: People and groups who set rules for you (boards of directors, state legislatures, health commissions, etc.)

e. Supplier publics: People who provide you with goods, supplies, services, etc. (utility companies, office supplies, newspapers, etc.)

Please note that a public you identify (Gloria Dei Luthern Church) has many smaller publics inside of it (choir, church council, circles, Sunday School, general members, members' spouses who do not belong themselves, clergy, etc.). Obviously the list of publics and publics inside them, can go on forever. In Chapter 2 we will explore ways to identify publics and how critical it is to do so.

MARKET: A market is an identified public with whom you decide you wish to establish a trade relationship. To put it into simpler terms: They have what you need/want

Of a list of 100 publics, you may find a half dozen that *could* meet your need if they choose to do so. The trick is *having* a list of publics from which to choose. . . . Without it I find groups suffer from "resource myopia," never realizing how many potential resources are available to them!

Example: You need printing done for a two color brochure. From your publics list you recognize the following who, physically, are capable of providing the brochures: newspapers, printing firms, print shops at local high schools, college or business print shops, etc.

EXCHANGE RELATIONSHIP: This is the keystone of success as it is the "bargain" that is struck between your group and the markets who have what you desire. It is the essence of marketing— THE TRADE OF VALUE FOR VALUE. Its qualities include:

1. Honesty and fairness.

2. No hidden agendas or pitfalls.

3. A user-oriented position.

4. A targeted approach.

5. Highest concern for what the other party will receive of value.

6. Attention to your agency's *success* in attaining goals.

7. A lot of homework!

HOW MARKETING IN NON-PROFITS
DIFFERS FROM THE BUSINESS WORLD

In the business world marketing concerns itself with one market—the customer.

Non-profits have a much more complex agenda, however, as they must deal with:

1. Clients

2. Volunteers

3. Donors

In measuring success, businesses simply calculate whether or not their profit and sales are better than their competitors.

It is not that simple for non-profits which must somehow measure whether or not they have reached:

1. Their goals for *service*. (Is it the *number* of clients reached or the *quality* of the service that counts?)

2. Their goals for funding. (Even when fundraising dollars are down, there is value in additional public awareness of the cause, more volunteers involved, contacts with potential key donors, and/or new program ideas.)

3. Their goals for volunteers. (How can you measure the future quality of volunteers in years to come?)

HOW NON-PROFIT MARKETING
IS SIMILAR TO BUSINESS MARKETING

There are more similarities than differences between the two worlds of business and non-profits. They include:

1. A need for organized "publics" information (written plans and procedures to gather information data.)

2. A base (through records, etc.) of data on demographics, donors, volunteers, etc.

3. A need for sound management of programs and production.

4. A need to develop the right *PRODUCT,* support it with the right *PROMOTION,* put it in the right *PLACE* and at the right *PRICE.* Please note that some translation will need to be made into acceptable language for volunteer programs, for example:

a. Product translates to "SERVICE," "INFORMATION," etc.

b. Promotion translates to "RECRUITMENT CAMPAIGN," "NEWS RELEASES," "SPEAKER'S BUREAU," "PR," etc.

c. Place translates to "LOCATION," "SERVICE DELIVERY AREA," "PUBLICS," "AUDIENCES," etc.

d. Price translates to "VOLUNTEER TIME DEMANDS," "ENERGY," and real costs (for out of pocket expenses, tickets, dues, etc.)

5. Recognition of competition: There are more groups vying for support, information vehicles, donors, volunteers, grant money, etc. making the non-profit, voluntary sector highly competitive. As a consultant and trainer dealing with hundreds of groups. I see those who are *not* using a marketing orientation falling by the wayside as they continue to deny that they are in a competitive business!

In an article from *Banker's Monthly Magazine,* March 1975, George Wasem, president of Commercial National Management Consulting Co. said, "Competition isn't limited to the private sector. Non-profits also operate in a very competitive environment."[4]

To understand just how accurate Wasem's words are, consider:
—There are 6 million organizations in the voluntary sector.
—350,000 religious groups
—37,000 human service organizations
—6,000 museums
—5,500 private libraries
—4,600 secondary schools
—3,500 hospitals
—1,500 colleges
—1,100 symphony orchestras[5]
That all adds up to COMPETITION folks!

6. A need for strategizing is a commonality between business and non-profits though few of the latter use this tool. Two strategies that could be used heavily are:

a. "Heavy user" concept that identifies key donors, volunteers, etc. and targets appeals toward them. This approach is usually much more fruitful than the normal scatter-gun tactic (often received by people as an "anyone-will-do" approach).

b. "Differentiation" concept that underscores a need for different approaches to different markets. While National Director for a large international health care agency I realized this need as appeals for support were tailored in language and information to churches, the medical profession, educators. etc. Unfortunately today I find many groups who are not aware of the need for tailoring their approach to their audience and blindly use pre-prepared materials created on New York's Madison Avenue that simply have no relevance to potential donors or volunteers in Wichita, Kansas, or Washington, Illinois.

The greatest similarity between business and non-profits is one of the critical need for a full-agency commitment to the marketing orientation. Without the support, for example, of the administration of your program to the use of marketing as a basic tool, there is little, if any, hope for success. Likewise, if the administration is sold on marketing but program directors refuse to accept its validity, again the chance for success is remote.

CONCLUSION

To put marketing in terms acceptable to the non-profit or voluntary sector, there must be:

1. Concern for changing needs of clients.

2. Processes that make it easy for people to make inquiries, suggestions, and share complaints, or opinions.

3. A commitment and the means to regularly survey people's needs, wants, feelings, motivations, etc.

4. Acceptance of clients, donors, and volunteers as partners, involving them in decisions that affect them.

5. Commitment to the "user oriented" philosophy of marketing that cares deeply about the values received by clients, volunteers, and donors in exchange for what they offer the agency or program.

6. Continual education of people as to how to use marketing as a tool for success.

Edward McKay, long time marketing consultant, is quoted by Phillip Kotler in his book *Marketing for Non-Profit Organizations*[6] and shares this advice for groups considering a change to a marketing orientation:

"It may require drastic and upsetting changes in organization. It usually demands new approaches to planning. It may set in motion a series of appraisals that will disclose surprising weaknesses in performance, distressing needs for modification of operating practices, and unexpected gaps, conflicts, or obsolescence in basic policies. Without doubt, it will call for reorientation of business philosophy and for the reversal of some long established attitudes. These changes will not be easy to implement. Objectives, obstacles, resistance, and deeprooted habits will have to be overcome."

CHAPTER I — REFERENCES

1. Kotler, Phillip. *Marketing For Non-Profit Organizations,* Prentice-Hall, 1975.
2. Ibid.
3. Wilson, Marlene. *The Effective Management of Volunteer Programs,* Volunteer Management Associates, 1977.
4. Montana, Patrick, G. *Marketing In Non-Profit Organizations,* Amacom, 1978.
5. Ibid., p. 56
6. Kotler, Phillip. *Marketing For Non-Profit Organizations,* Prentice-Hall, 1975.
7. Sargent, Alice. *The Androgynons Manager,* Amacom, 1981.

CHAPTER II

Where To Begin—Step 1
What Do You Have?

"It is necessary therefore it is possible."
. . . Abraham Maslow

When instituting a marketing orientation for your volunteer program, it is vital that you understand the four-step process that will bring success.

As I travel around the country, training people in marketing, management, and resource development, I find that they have rarely identified these steps which are:

#1. What do you *HAVE?*

#2. What do you *NEED?*

#3. *WHO HAS* what you need?

#4. *HOW DO YOU GET* what you need?

In most instances, people begin with step #2—their *need*—and then find themselves with many problems, including resource myopia.

It is interesting to note that the same groups, who would never think of writing a check for a purchase without first looking at their bank account balance, do exactly that by attempting to fill a need without knowing what resources they have in hand!

WHAT BUSINESS ARE YOU IN?

In every training session I conduct, there is one exercise I have the audience do. It is to write down a one sentence statement on what business they think their agency or program is in.

It is interesting to see the strange looks I get when I first assign that task. Most people give me a cocked-eyebrow, "EVERYONE *knows* what-we-do!" look and proceed to jot their answer down, then stare all-knowingly at me.

I throw them a curve, however, when I ask them to compare their answer to others from their agency and then with a stranger to compare perceptions.

It then becomes my turn to cock an eyebrow when they discover two things:

1. Others from their agency often have a different definition of what business they are in, and

2. Strangers are not clear at all on what they do.

At that point I'm always reminded of the dear soul from Texas who was irate because she felt she's been rejected by a Meals-On-Wheels program after devising a new system for meal delivery.

She explained that she had just retired after a life long career as a time-study engineer and had spent hours on a new system that would allow her local program to package and deliver meals 60% more efficiently.

"Why," she said, "I had it down to just seven minutes per meal from the time a volunteer rang the bell of the recipient's home to when they left!"

As she spoke I had a mental image of the Meals-On-Wheels volunteers rushing past the recipients as they answered their doors, flinging the food on the kitchen table, ripping off the foil as they shouted, *"EAT! EAT!"* and racing back past the astonished person in a dash for their cars!

This very hurt and confused volunteer, who had offered her talents honestly, was a victim of an inaccurate perception of what the program *really* was—what business it was in.

She thought the business was feeding people—when really their business is personal interaction with people who are home-bound and often alone. The food is simply the vehicle to accomplish the greater goal.

Groups that complain of recruitment, fund-raising, or volunteer-staff problems, etc. are in reality, often suffering from the result of mixed, clouded, narrow, or outdated ideas about their purpose.

When hospitals realized they were in the wellness business rather than sickness business a whole new world opened up to them with new programs, PR, recruitment, and resource development avenues.

The same is true for the American Cancer Society when they realized they were in the business of HOPE, not disease. And all manner of new ways to help and support opened up when churches began to realize they were in the business of human fellowship not just doctrine and stained glass!

AN EXERCISE TO IDENTIFY PURPOSE

1. Gather your key people together—insure a mixture of paid staff, volunteers, board members, clients, and administrators.

2. Ask them to write down what business they think your agency is in. Do the same for your volunteer program or department.

3. On a blackboard or large paper, compare the answers.

4. Do not shoot anyone down. Their perspective may help you understand misconceptions and confusion.

5. Agree on a single definition and urge participants to project (to other staff, recruits, the public, etc.) this singular definition.

---

*AN OPEN AGREEMENT OF WHAT BUSINESS YOU ARE IN IS CRITICAL FOR MARKETING, TO INSURE A CLEAR PICTURE FOR POTENTIAL CLIENTS, VOLUNTEERS, AND SUPPORTERS.

WHAT'S YOUR PRODUCT

Every organization produces a "product" of at least one of the following. For volunteer programs there is often a mixture of "products" to be offered:

1. *Physical products*—books, pins, banners, fundraising items, re-sale goods, etc.

2. *Services*—health care, counseling, information, youth development, education, relief, etc.

3. *Persons*—political candidates, stronger image of profession, etc.

4. *Organizations*—memberships, collaborations, associations, unions, etc.

5. *Ideas*—birth control, substance abuse education, crime prevention, environmental protection, religious convictions, safety, etc.

THREE "PRODUCT" CLASSIFICATIONS

In marketing circles products are classified in three ways[1] that have great significance for volunteer programs when translated to our terminology:

THE EXPECTED PRODUCT—defined as a customer's *minimum* expectations concerning price, delivery, technical support, etc.

For volunteer programs this can be translated into the expectations volunteers have when they offer their energies to work with you:

1. "Price"—What it will "cost" them in out of pocket expenses, energy, and emotional drain.

2. "Delivery"—When, where, and how they expect they will have to perform their duties.

3. "Technical Support"—How they will be trained to carry out assignments, who will help them, who will oversee their efforts, how the other staff, especially paid, will work with them.

*IT IS CRITICAL TO UNCOVER THE VOLUNTEER'S EXPECTATIONS *PRIOR* TO WORKING, TO COMPARE THEM TO REALITY!

THE AUGMENTED PRODUCT—Defined as offering the customer *more* than they expected or think they need.

In volunteer programs this can be translated into a volunteer's feeling that they are exceeding their minimum expectations by receiving the added value of knowing they are truly making a difference, building skills, feeling needed, having their efforts recorded for their resume, and/or simply having fun.

The wise volunteer director keeps a close tab on this augmentation, being aware of the dozens of "benefits" that might be offered to volunteers in order that they feel good about their work, tell others, and stay longer.

The only "danger" in augmentation is that these additional benefits may begin to be regarded as normal, thus setting up higher expectations for future volunteer work.

THE POTENTIAL PRODUCT—This is defined as everything feasible that can be done to attract and retain customers.

In volunteer programs this translates to an awareness of potential benefits that can be offered in conjunctiion with various volunteer assignments. These are then advertised in the recruitment process *and* their delivery insured (never promise what you can't deliver!) for retention purposes.

A look at the reasons people volunteer, as listed in chapter #4, will start you thinking as to potential benefits, and an informal survey of your present volunteers and what they "get" from their efforts will expand this list.

AN EXERCISE IN PRODUCT IDENTIFICATION

It is critical for your program that you identify and list your "products." YOU CANNOT MARKET "PRODUCTS" IF YOU DON'T KNOW WHAT THEY ARE!

1. In a brainstorming session with people from several perspectives (paid staff, volunteers, administration, board, clients) identify your program's "products." Note expected, augmented and potential aspects.

2. List benefits of each product.

3. List target publics who could use each "product."

4. Prioritize your products by importance to your group— in other words, where you plan to spend most of your developmental dollars and energies.

5. Devise plans to insure that all new people, paid or non-paid, who come to work in your program, understand your products and their prioritization.

WHAT BUSINESS DOES THE PUBLIC THINK YOU'RE IN?
WHAT PRODUCTS DO THEY THINK YOU OFFER?

It is important that you assess perceptions of people *outside* your immediate circle to test the accuracy of their perceptions as to what business you are in and what products you offer. Many people still think 4-H & Extension only deals with livestock sales; that Girl Scouts only teach girls how to camp and that YWCA's simply run rooming houses! If you find that your image is cloudy, STOP! and do all you can to clarify it. A cloudy or totally inaccurate perception by the public or other agencies will prevent potential volunteers, clients, and supporters from coming to you. It will also attract people for the wrong reasons—setting up a false expectation in their minds of what involvement with you will bring. This is very dangerous—much like storing poison in a pop bottle or sleeping pills in a candy jar!

AN EXERCISE TO UNCOVER PERCEPTIONS

1. Identify several broad-based community groups with whom you have an "inside" contact. (Women's Clubs, churches, Rotary, County Health Services, etc.)

2. Prepare a one-page, multiple choice questionnaire to find out what people think you do and what products you offer.

3. Distribute and administer.

4. Tabulate results and report back to participating groups in conjunction with a crisp presentation on your program's offerings, needs, and purpose. (This then becomes a potential recruitment presentation to acquire volunteers or a fundraising effort to win support.)

5. Act on the survey results to correct misperceptions and/or strengthen accurate definitions.

If you feel the need to survey an entire area, you might try to enlist banks, utility companies, and local businesses who mail to your total area regularly to assist you. A survey tucked in with monthly statements and returned with payments will "blanket" an area, cost you no postage and be processed efficiently. In exchange for this service the cooperating business receives recognition for community service, positive publicity, and a possible tax deduction. (Trading value for value!)

ANALYZING YOUR MARKET

Before deciding on what market to target for your efforts (recruitment, fundraising, support, etc.) you must conduct a marketing analysis in order to insure the greatest chance at success by identifying people interested in your offerings.

The marketing analysis is made up of two parts:[2] 1) The marketing structure analysis, and 2) Consumer analysis. Let's look at both, putting them into words we can understand for volunteer programs.

MARKETING STRUCTURE ANALYSIS—
BREAKING LIFE DOWN INTO BITE-SIZED BITS!

Since all of the population is your potential market (everyone *could* volunteer in some measure!) you will need to look at the smaller parts of the whole to determine which you will target.

This is what a market structure analysis is—an examination of the parts of the whole. This analysis is made up of four steps:

1. *Market Definition*—the definition of the boundaries of a market, knowing that not everyone wants to work with seniors, or coach little leaguers, or support environmental issues, etc. In this effort you will want to identify individuals who *already* have an interest or sensitivity to what you offer through services. Such people might be: parents of children you serve; those with goals that dovetail with yours (i.e.: environmentalists would be a natural market for a volunteer program for a forest preserve); clients who have used your agency services; retired teachers for school volunteer programs, etc.

2. *Market Segmentation*—after defining people potentially interested in involvement with you, it becomes necessary to divide these publics into homogeneous groups. This might mean the members of a women's club that are interested in your cause or a church that has expressed interest in involvement. In identifying the segments, you are really just trying to zero in on those groups that are most likely to give you the highest response

and resource potential. In other words, your "best shot" at a successful relationship. You might want to "segment" markets in your mind by associations or groups, age, education, vocation or avocation, church membership, geography, income, etc.

3. *Market Positioning*—this comes after careful study that identifies a special niche in which to locate and let your uniqueness (differentiation) shine! For a park district, this might mean seeing that in the community there are tons of volunteer programs for youth but almost none for seniors or handicapped, and proceeding to develop and staff such programs. This effort makes these programs unique in their services and would lead the effective volunteer manager to recruit volunteers from groups with high interest in seniors and handicapped.

4. *Market Orchestration*—the fourth step of the marketing structure analysis harmonizes all of the marketing to different segments. It is important to decide what different markets are to be approached, to decide what percent of your total marketing efforts will be assigned to each, and to synchronize efforts so they work together. During this coordination process, different approaches may be mapped out for each segments, but all are still synchronized so they do not affect each other negatively. The orchestration of time allotment needs to have a degree of flexibility to it, so that if one market becomes more fruitful than the others, you can shift a larger percentage of your energies to its cultivation. (Example: your program was giving 20% of its energies to gaining support from the local Junior Women's Club. The club president gets so enthusiastic she helps you win the support of the 20 other clubs in your area. Obviously, it's time to shift more energies to this fruitful arena.)

THE CONSUMER ANALYSIS—WHO NEEDS WHAT?

In marketing terms, this is simply defined as the process by which the needs, perceptions, preferences, and satisfactions of potential markets (groups, individuals, donors, volunteers, etc.) are tracked.

It is vital to the relevancy of volunteer programs that they constantly measure and remeasure how the "consumer" (volunteer, donor, client, etc.) *feels* about the program or agency. It is critical to remember that feelings are facts and not discount them simply to justify actions.

In working with groups across the country, I run into those that complain of recruitment, PR, funding, and support woes. In looking into these ills, however, I often find they are symptoms of a deeper problem—a group offering programs/services that are no longer needed or wanted.

One group, that suffered from an acute case of this "out-of-touch" malady, confessed that they had stopped surveying their markets "because they kept bad-mouthing what we do, and we just decided they were stupid!"

The *purpose* of any consumer survey is to keep in touch. The *challenge* is to respond to what you're told, avoiding any defensiveness or "yeah-but" responses!

AN EXERCISE TO ANALYZE
YOUR CONSUMER MARKETS

1. With input from as many varied perspectives as possible, devise ways to "survey" various market segments.

2. Brainstorm specific questions, such as:

   a. "How enjoyable is it to work as a volunteer with this group? Why?" (vol.)

   b. "Is the volunteer job meeting needs you have? What are they?" (vol.)

   c. "Where could the volunteer department improve?" (vol.)

   d. "Why did you choose to volunteer with us rather than other groups?" (vol.)

   e. "What will keep you coming back?" (vol.)

   f. "What could drive you away?" (vol.)

   g. "Who do you think is ultimately helped by what you do?" (donor/vol.)

   h. "How effective do you feel the help given by this agency is for clients?" (donor/vol.)

   i. "Why do you give your dollars to us?" "Where do you think the money goes?" (donor)

j. "Should we continue the XXX fundraising event in the future? What new ideas should be tried?" (donor)

k. "How much does the agency really help people? (all)

3. Develop ways to survey groups and individuals.

    a. In written form—short, easy to read, simple way to return.

    b. In verbal form—phone surveys, interviews, etc.

    c. In public form—newspapers, fliers, inserts in mailers, etc.

    The first two are targeted approaches, the last is scatter-gun and usually renders a new perspective—one that is valuable but different.

4. Administer the survey, tabulating and reporting results.

5. Compare with information gathered in surveys suggested previously ("AN EXERCISE TO UNCOVER PERCEPTIONS) and work into planning.

DIFFERENTIATION—WHAT MAKES YOU SPECIAL?

Sometime when you have a minute, look at a list of all the clubs, churches, schools, agencies, and programs in your area that offer volunteer opportunities. The list will probably seem endless and should cause you to understand what a competitive business you are in!

As you look at the list, ask yourself:

1. What sets your program apart?

2. Why would people choose to work with you rather than any of the others?

3. What do you offer that can attract and keep volunteers?

4. How do you tell people about your uniqueness? (These same questions can apply to client appeal, fundraising, support, advocacy, etc.)

Theodore Levitt, in his book *The Marketing Imagination*[3] tells us: "Sellers use differentation to make their expected, augmented, and potential products stand out from their competitions."

If marketing is about anything, it is about getting the public to correctly differentiate what you do, how you do it, and what you offer.

FIVE FACTORS TO CONSIDER
THAT MIGHT MAKE YOU DIFFERENT

To determine what might make you special in the minds of potential volunteers, donors, etc. you might consider these five factors:[4]

1. *Durability*—How long will your "product" or opportunity last? How stable is your agency or service?

2. *Complexity*—How complicated is it to work with you and your "product"? Are there many different levels to offer people—so that there is a mixture of simple, moderate and complex assignments available?

3. *Visibility*—How conspicuous is your "product" or volunteer opportunity?

4. *Risk*—How risky is it to work with you?

5. *Familiarity*—How familiar is the work? Something done all the time (talk on phone) or a whole new task (using a computer).

You will probably have great success in recruiting volunteers if your involvement opportunities are stable (durability), easy to do (complexity), visible, fun (low risk), and highly familiar! An example of such a job might be serving as hosts four times a year for popular community theater productions.

As there is more open competition for volunteers, I find that those programs which attend carefully to sound volunteer management principles (offering sound planning, explicit job designs, good training, positive supervision, etc.) are those that stand head and shoulders above the rest. These principles speak to low risk and complexity and offer greater potential for personal success and rewards.

Differentiation is a constant factor in marketing of products and services as witnessed in the fight for customers that is presently going on between telephone systems. In this race for the top market share, A. T. & T. is basing their appeal on what makes them *different* from the rest. In the mad scramble for a share of the computer market, Apple made a giant leap in sales when they called their product "a personal computer" to differentiate it from a business computer that requires an expert to run it.

AN EXERCISE IN DIFFERENTIATION

1. In a brainstorming session with as many varied perspectives as possible, list the benefits, qualities, etc. that make you different:

   a. programatically

   b. historically

   c. in offering volunteer opportunities

   d. philosophically

   e. in how you support your work

2. List other community groups that provide similar or like services. What makes you different?

3. List the largest volunteer programs in your area that are at least in the same category of service (health, education, environmental, youth, etc.). What differentiates what you offer volunteers?

This same principle of differentiation needs to be applied to volunteer programs as they scramble for their share of the volunteer energy bank! Only those who use this marketing tool to their advantage will prosper and grow.

DIFFERENTIATION AND YOUR AGENT PUBLICS

It is critical for you to identify those publics that can speak in your program's behalf, referring people to you and to then insure that these public "agents" understand your differentiation.

Through personal contacts, insure that your Voluntary Action Center, Council of Churches, school offices, city officials, human service referral agencies, R.S.V.P.'s, Chamber of Commerce, service clubs, etc. know what you do, how you do it, what benefits are offered volunteers, and how you are unique.

IDENTIFYING YOUR PUBLICS, or:
"Is Anybody Out There?"

As discussed in Chapter One, marketing has three major components: PUBLICS, MARKETS, and EXCHANGE RELATIONSHIPS.

Understanding *publics* is the first step toward success and is often an omitted one for volunteer programs.

WHAT IS A PUBLIC?

A public is an identifiable segment of society that can be categorized in your mind either by generic quality (young boys, ages 8-10) or title (Cub Scouts, Pack 12). You *might* have an exchange relationship with them in the future, but you don't know that for sure.

As stated in Chapter I *every* identifiable group that surrounds you is a public, so the list can be quite lengthy when you begin to record them! To complicate it further, publics themselves have smaller publics within their structure (i.e.: a school is a public with many internal publics such as the band, teachers, pupils, student council, etc.).

CATEGORIES OF PUBLICS

Let's review the four categories of publics as introduced in Chapter 1:

1. *Input*—those publics which provide you with services, goods, control, etc. For a church this would be:

    a. Council of Churches, denomination hierarchy (*"Regulatory"* Input Public)

    b. members, donors, etc. (*"Support"* Input Publics)

    c. pew makers, hymnal companies, etc. (*"Supplier"* Input Publics)

2. *Internal Publics*—part of an organization's internal composition. In the church that might mean:

    a. clergy, members, choir, etc.

3. *Agent Publics*—publics that speak in behalf of the organization, both officially and unofficially—often the best "recruiters".

    a. members, clergy, Welcome Wagon hostesses, Council of Churches' secretary, etc. (*"Referral"* Publics, including those people outside the church who refer people there)

4. *Consuming Publics*—those people and groups who use the services of the organization:

    a. members, non-members using the day care, Boy Scout troops, etc. (*"Client"* Consuming Publics)

b. community people who get information from the church, media, etc. *("General"* Consuming Public)

Please note that volunteers can exist in all categories, acting at different times as clients, agents, regulators, suppliers, support, and in-house publics!

AN EXERCISE TO TRACK PUBLICS

1. In a brain storming session of people from many perspectives, think of as many "publics" as possible and write them on a large piece of paper (butcher paper, newsprint, etc.) The previous list of publics may help people think of ones to add.

2. Stimulate thinking by suggesting categories (schools, churches, businesses, clubs, etc.) and ask people to name specifics for each. A telephone directory, club and business lists from the Chamber of Commerce, churches and school directories, city offices list, etc. would be helpful.

3. DO NOT EXCLUDE ANY GROUP because you think "they wouldn't help us" or "they're too obscure", that's not an issue. Simply list as many publics as possible.

4. Don't overlook generic groupings (seniors, school kids, clients, past volunteers, pet owners, etc.)

5. When you have thought of all the publics you can, put your large paper, now filled out with hundreds of publics, in a conspicuous spot on your site.

6. Challenge everyone who comes by the chart to think of more publics and add to the list.

7. Make this on-going exercise fun! Possibly keep a bowl of life-savers or candy kisses near the chart, inviting everyone who adds a public to help themselves.

8. Select a volunteer with great organizational (left-brained!) skills to transfer the information on the chart to individual cards and place them in a "resource file" by category for easy retrieval. If you have access to a computer, all this information can be stored on discs.

THE RESOURCE FILE

The purpose of this "resource file" of publics is to help you, when at any point, you identify specific needs of your program. At that point you can check your file to identify publics who have what you want/need.

This process, of *first* identifying who/what you have around you, prevents resource myopia and broadens your thinking. Example: you find you need 100, 3-color posters in two months. If you do *not* have a publics chart, the natural tendency is to consult the yellow pages of your phone book and call for bids.

With a publics chart you realize that several publics *could* do this printing for you: print shops at public and vocational high schools, a large business, local newspapers, art display firms, and the local department store. Your next step is to identify contacts with any of these publics and work to establish an exchange relationship to get your posters.

IDENTIFYING CONTACTS INSIDE PUBLICS—
The People Connection!

The second, and most important, step in identifying publics is recognition of personal contacts you have *inside* those publics.

As people come past your publics chart, challenge them to share with you any contacts they have for each public. They can jot this information down under each public, telling:

1. Their own name and phone number
2. The date (to know how current information is)
3. Their contact person and position

Example: Under O'Neill Jr. High might be: "Sue Vineyard—555-1111, husband Wes teaches art—8/84" and "Tippy Coats—555-2635, son Jeff is Student Council Pres.—1/85"

These contacts, or authenticators, are added to the file on each public, thus creating a resource inventory with available contacts for hundreds of diverse publics that surround you.

THE COMPLETE RESOURCE INVENTORY FILE

Let's stop a moment to look at this resource inventory file. It needs to be an easy to use, practical data piece—either on a 5x7 index card, or if you have such access, computerized.

Information to be included for *titled* groups:

1. Name, address, phone
2. Group purpose (or business product)
3. Chief officers, titles, and term lengths
4. Published creed if available
5. Involvement with volunteer programs in past (yours and others)
6. Financial information (if available)—Fiscal year boundaries
7. Meeting times/places or business hours
8. Information on internal structure
9. Contacts you have inside—name/date/phone/title, etc.
10. Comments

Don't panic when you look at the 10 information categories above— for the vast number of publics you won't have much more than a group title. It is when you decide they might become a *market* that you may wish to add the more detailed information!

Also understand that all of this information will not be available immediately, but will be added through time and contacts inside the groups. Newly added contacts listed on your Publics Chart will help expand your information.

This file needs to be updated regularly and cross-filed by categories of interest to you.

Information to be included for *generic* groups:

1. Name (seniors, high school youth, etc.)
2. Lists of groups concerned with their issues (AARP, RSVP, scouting, etc.)
3. Programs offered for this public
4. Contacts you have into this group—names, etc.

When these files are available and being used, your program will be well on its way to getting what you need/want through publics that surround you.

AN INTERNAL RESOURCE FILE:
Discovering Backyard Riches!

Before we move on, let's explore the development of one more rich resource—that found in your own "backyard." This internal file will help you track, discover, and develop the human, physical, and emotional resources at hand.

HUMAN RESOURCES: The Gifts People Have

Ask your paid and non-paid staff (volunteers) to list groups to which they belong, volunteer and leadership experiences they have had, training, work and/or business experiences, hobbies, etc. Also ask them to list any publications for each of their groups. Through this effort you will probably discover skills and contacts you never knew existed in people you see regularly!

Remember that in the Gallup Poll on Volunteerism conducted in 1982,[5] people who said they were *willing* to volunteer but were *not* doing so explained that their non-involvement came because NO ONE ASKED THEM! When we know the rich experiential background of a person, we have a better idea of what to ask of them, allowing them to share their gifts and feel appreciated.

PHYSICAL RESOURCES

Another resource inventory, that can be beneficial when it comes time to establishing exchange relationships, lists all of the physical assets you have. Remember that the building you use 9-5, Monday-Friday, and probably think little about, might be an incredible gift to the rapidly growing computer club that meets each Saturday. If sharing the building can be arranged *and* you need computerization for your inventory files—you may just have a potential exchange of value for value!

Look around you—begin a list of physical assets: building, parking lot, equipment, communication vehicles, library of books, training opportunities, etc. etc. Discount *nothing!* What you take for granted that "everyone has" may be the item some other group longs for! For example, an art club that could provide you with the 100 posters you need may do so in exchange for the use of your building for their monthly meetings or your parking lot on a weekend which can become the site of their annual art show.

EMOTIONAL RESOURCES

One last resource is often overlooked—that of the feelings and interpersonal resources you might offer to people in exchange for their efforts. We will discuss more of this in Chapter 4 when we look into motivation, but it is good to also mention it here, so that you will link the recognition of these assets with the human and physical ones.

Emotional resources might include:

1. Your positive reputation—attracting people who want to be associated with success and positivity.
2. Fun—people can associate good times with your program.
3. High visibility—people know they will be seen by many people when working with you.
4. Socialization—people can make friends/contacts through you.
5. Association—people can get to know community leaders and even celebrities by working with you.
6. Status—people can gain status with you.
7. Gifts—people can use their gifts and talents with you that they cannot use elsewhere.
8. Feeling needed—a self perception that is worth its weight in gold!
9. Recognition—people will be rewarded for their work with you.

Although these factors can be more difficult to track than physical assets or human resources, they are none the less valuable as they deal with organizational climate—how it "feels" to be associated with your program.

In the final analysis it is these feelings that will either retain or eject your volunteers, donors, supporters, etc.

MAPPING DEMANDS ON YOUR PROGRAM

On examining what you have, it is critical that you have an understanding of all of the demands made on your program in terms of energies, time frames, and complexities.

Too frequently I see groups trying to institute marketing efforts during time periods when there are a thousand other demands placed on them—combinations that usually spell disaster. An intense volunteer recruitment campaign should never be planned at the time the volunteer director is trying to work on budgets, prepare final reports, and advocate for new programs. A large fundraiser should not be scheduled during the summer when more volunteers and paid staff vacation.

AN EXERCISE TO MAP YOUR DEMANDS

1. Get a *large* twelve month calendar
2. Using various colors fill in:
   a. administrative demands
   b. volunteer functions
   c. major holidays (religious, national, state, etc.)
   d. school holidays
   e. projects and events of program and agency including time it takes for development.
   f. United Way campaign dates
   g. community events that could impact you
   h. competing events of other major agencies and groups in your area

---

Keep this calendar updated and in plain sight for everyone to see. It reminds everyone of times of high energy demands and opportunities to catch a breath or two!

A pattern will probably emerge that shows when efforts for marketing of any nature (recruitment, fundraising, advocacy, etc.) need to be made *or* avoided. Try to balance your demand calendar as much as possible; it will spread energies more evenly and probably do a great deal to prevent burnout—yours and others!

Be aware that volunteers tend to "gear-up" in late August, September and January. Summer months are for vacations and kids—not volunteering! Seniors volunteer with seasons in mind as they flee extremes of weather. Take all these factors into consideration as you assess demands.

AN EXTERNAL RESOURCE INVENTORY!

After completing your internal audit, it becomes necessary to look at external factors that impact and support your program. Areas of interest include demographics, help, and trends.

DEMOGRAPHICS INFORMATION: Who's Out There and How Tall Are They?

Well, maybe you really don't need to know people's heights, but you *do* need to know some basic statistics about the people that surround you, so you can take this information into consideration in marketing plans.

Your local Chamber of Commerce, town hall, the Census Bureau, etc. can provide the figures you need regarding:

1. Average age of population
2. Income
3. Employment/unemployment
4. Religious affiliations
5. Languages
6. Education
7. Population trends (increasing? decreasing?) etc.

It would be vital to know, for instance, the average age in a community before designing volunteer jobs. I would design and recruit very differently in Tampa, Florida (average age: 57) and Boulder, Colorado (average age: 26)! I would design fundraising campaigns differently in DuPage County, Illinois, where unemployment is 2%, than in areas of West Virginia, where unemployment is 35%.

44

WHAT HELP IS AVAILABLE . . .

One of the emerging trends in human services and volunteerism is the networking that is beginning to happen. A realization seems to be dawning that groups can no longer afford to "re-invent the wheel," but instead must begin to share their resources, ideas, and solutions to problems.

At one time, groups jealously guarded "their" volunteers, fundraising ideas, programs, and ideas, much like Coca Cola guards its soft drink formula!

Today, volunteer directors find their counterparts more than willing to share ideas and learnings through such organized efforts as:

1. DOVIA'S—(Directors of Volunteers In Agencies). This is not a nationally organized association but a common title for spontaneous groups of people who oversee volunteer efforts in local communities. Often informal, these groups meet monthly or so to discuss commonalities, share support, ideas, resources. The more formalized DOVIA'S have scheduled programs with people, such as myself, Marlene Wilson, Susan Ellis, Ivan Scheier, etc., coming in to train. Dr. Scheier has produced the only DOVIA Directory[6] which can lead you to groups in your area or offer possible contact information as you seek to set up your own DOVIA.

2. V.A.C.'S (Voluntary Action Centers) or Volunteer Centers: There are hundreds of VACs in the U.S. and Canada with the general purpose of screening volunteers for placement in local agencies and programs. In addition to this function, many VACs develop and manage programs of their own, such as the offering of training, research, etc. A directory of VACs can be obtained through VOLUNTEER, 1111 N. 19th Street, Suite 500, Arlington, Virginia 22209 if you cannot locate one through your phone book. I urge all volunteer administrators to make themselves and their programs known to the VAC and its Director so that volunteers can be obtained through this resource (AGENT PUBLIC), and any support groups of volunteer directors can be contacted through the VAC.

3. National/International Groups: There is a danger in beginning to name groups because you can never name them all! I'll risk anger by those omitted because the value of at least knowing

three is better than nothing. I urge you to pursue other existing groups on your own or through the guidance of my first book: *Finding Your Way Through The Maze of Volunteer Management* which lists hundreds of groups, associations, books, periodicals, services, and resources in 68 categories from "Arts" to "Youth."[7] "Maze" was my first attempt to make people aware of the help that is at hand in our field.

Three major groups specializing in a different segment of the volunteer market that can serve as excellent resources are:

a. *The Association of Volunteer Administration* (AVA) is a professional association for people (paid or non-paid) who administer volunteers. Over 1100 members represent every conceivable type and size of program. AVA sponsors the annual (October) National Conference on Volunteerism, publishes *The Journal of Volunteer Administration,* offers competency-based certification (the C.V.A.) and regional conferences open to all volunteer directors. AVA national headquarters is P.O. Box 4584, Boulder, Colorado 80306 (303) 497-0238.

b. VOLUNTEER, *The National Center for Citizen Involvement* is a group which seeks to serve the needs of volunteers and groups that serve them. It is a membership organization run by a paid staff and offers training, annual conferences, the magazine "Voluntary Action Leadership," books related to volunteerism through its "Volunteer Readership" sales catalogue, recognition items etc. VOLUNTEER can be reached at 1111 N. 19th Street, Suite 500, Arlington, Virginia 22209 (703) 276-0542.

c. *Independent Sector* is a Washington, D. C. based group that concerns itself with the broad area of voluntarism with special interest in advocacy, cooperation between factors in all sectors, legislation and corporate involvement. It commissioned the Gallup Organization to gather the latest statistics on volunteerism for its publication *Americans Volunteer.* It also provides consultation, an annual convention, and publications of interest to people involved in voluntary development. Independent Sector is located at 1828 L. Street, N.W., Washington, D.C. 20036.

4. Cause-based organizations exist, such as ASDVS (for Directors of Volunteer Services in Hospitals) and NAVCJ (for Volunteers in Criminal Justice) and are best tracked through your own journals, information channels, etc. In addition to these, many groups that support your cause, such as those supporting community theaters, environmental issues, etc. are offering training, assistance, etc. for the volunteer issues impacting their groups. Again, locating these groups can best come through your own channels.

5. Specific training for volunteer administrators is offered more and more as groups and individuals identify their need for learning. As mentioned previously, many local VACs, DOVIAS etc. may offer training as well as that offered through national groups at conventions and meetings.

One chapter of *Finding Your Way Through The Maze Of Volunteer Management* is devoted to training identified throughout the United States and contact information for each. The list cannot possibly be updated as regularly as changes occur (probably weekly!) and is not all-inclusive, so I urge you to seek out training most convenient to you.

One of the longest running and most highly regarded programs is headed by Marlene Wilson at the University of Colorado in Boulder and is broken into three week-long levels:

Level I: Basic management skills for volunteer directors (held in summer)

Level II: Interpersonal and high level administrative skills (held in winter)

Level III: Four speciality tracks—Training/Power/Conflict Resolution/Resources Development (held in fall)

(For further information: Univ. of Colorado, Department of Housing, Conferences, Campus Box 12559, Boulder, CO. 80310.)

TRENDS THAT SURROUND US

It is critical to understand the impact of the volunteer and general trends that surround us as they can and do alter plans of service delivery, recruitment and marketing. Let's examine the known trends of today:

VOLUNTEER TRENDS

For the first time in many years new insight was gathered on volunteering through the Gallup Poll on Volunteering[8] commissioned by Independent Sector.

It is critical that a clear and accurate picture of volunteering exists as efforts are made to recruit, contact, etc. people. In actuality, the Gallup Poll has provided a "consumer analysis" to be used in planning and implementing volunteer efforts.

The old stereotype of Polly-Do-Gooder the volunteer—white, female, well-educated but non-working, married, a mother of 2.5 children in school, affluent and living the good life in suburbia was rather shaken by the following facts:

1. People most likely to volunteer (63%) are working and have household incomes under $20,000.

2. 45% of volunteers are male.

3. 53% of adults identify themselves as volunteers.

4. 26% of Americans give 1-3 hours per week of volunteer work; 8% give 4-6 hours; 10% give 7 or more per week.

5. 91% of all volunteers have made charitable contributions compared to 66% among non-volunteers.

6. 66% of volunteers said they were doing the same or more volunteering than three years ago.

7. 28% of volunteers live in towns of populations under 2,500.

8. 52% of volunteers have a high school education or less.

9. 47% of volunteers have a household income under $20,000.

10. 17% of volunteers have incomes under $10,000.

11. Why people volunteer:
    a. 44%—asked directly
    b. 29%—because a loved one was involved
    c. 31%—through group participation
    d. 6%—ad or media information

12. Why people say "no" to volunteer:
    a. 46%—too busy
    b. 14%—health reasons

c. 18%—lack of interest

d. 8%—lack of time due to paid work

13. Why people who *would* volunteer, aren't:

"NO ONE ASKED!"

A close inspection of those facts shoots down old stereotypes; refutes the well-worn argument that there aren't enough volunteers any more because women have gone to work; shows that "volunteering" is not an exclusive suburban sport; and shows a correlation between giving and volunteering. I urge you to acquire the entire poll and see how many factors impact and influence *your* volunteer plans.

It is not unusual for groups, who call me in because they are having "recruitment" woes, discover through the study of factors that surround them, that they have been targeting their efforts inappropriately or not contacting the right people.

I feel the most telling pair of answers in the poll is that most people who *do* volunteer do so because they were asked, and those that would be willing to volunteer but are not doing so simply have *not* been asked. I see this as a mandate to recruiters to work harder to contact the right people!

GENERAL TRENDS

Several sources of information provide us with insight into the publics that surround our programs. Again, it is very important for you to understand the statistics that surround your work, not only for those efforts you are undertaking presently but for long-range planning.

1. 62% of Americans working are unhappy and dissatisfied with their paid work.[9] This can be translated into people eager to find satisfaction elsewhere—opening the door to voluntary organizations offering such fulfillment.

2. By 1990, 1 out of 8 people will be over 65.[10]

3. By 1990, there will be 6% reduction in people ages 16-24[11]

4. 43% of working women are single head of households.[12]

5. In 1979 only 14% of men were sole money earning heads of households (down from 70% in 1950.[13]

6. By 1990 there will be a 45% increase in people between ages 25-44. [14]

7. By 1990, 61% of all women over age 18 will work outside the home. [15]

MEGATRENDS

In his book *Megatrends*, [16] John Naisbitt outlines ten major trends that are already at work in America and having great impact on all facets of life, including volunteerism.

Naisbitt's work, which reflects the amount of attention given to major subjects in periodicals of the country, thus indicating "trends", is must reading for all volunteer directors as they plan their efforts and work with the modern volunteers.

The ten trends listed and some possible implications are:

MEGATREND	IMPLICATIONS
1. Shift from industrial to INFORMATIONAL society.	1. Demands clear communication— how easy it is to contact you? To know what volunteer work is available? To know what's expected? What avenues for feedback?
2. Shift from forced technology to HIGH TECH/ HIGH TOUCH.	1. Demand to work directly with people as volunteers are forced to deal with high tech in their life. Volunteering offers great opportunities to be in "people" business."
3. Move from national WORLD economy.	1. All things impact our programs; barter being used in world economy and coming to be accepted on local level. Must avoid isolationism.

50

4. Shift from short term to LONG RANGE thinking.

1. Need to devise 5 year plans for programs and plans to accomplish them; need to use marketing for long range results.

5. Move from centralization to DECENTRALIZATION.

1. Decisions need to be made at action level rather than in administrative offices; volunteers who deliver services can help plan most effectively.

6. Move from institutional to SELF-HELP.

1. Greatest gains in volunteerism are coming in self-help areas; need to explore programs of self-help; use of volunteers who are clients also.

7. Move from representative to PARTICIPATORY democracy.

1. This echos the demand most volunteers have to involve them in decisions that affect them!

8. Shift from hierarchies to NETWORKING.

1. Need to network with other programs to avoid duplication of services, learn from one another, share resources, shuttle skilled volunteers among groups, jointly advocate, etc.

9. Move from North to SOUTH.

1. Need to keep up to date on demographics and affect they will have on volunteer pool, client demand, etc.

10. Shift from either/or MULTIPLE options.

1. Need to build in flexibility in programs such as flextime, shared jobs, flexspace, seasonal work, etc.

AN EXERCISE TO DISCUSS TRENDS

1. Gather, in a relaxed setting if possible, key people from various perspectives of your program.

2. Prior to gathering ask them to read Naisbitt's *Megatrends* and a summary of volunteer and general trends you have put together.

3. Brainstorm implications for each as they affect program services, clients, volunteers, potential recruits, paid staff, planning, etc.

4. Examine goals, objectives, plans of action, and job designs for your program in light of implications discussed.

5. Make adjustments as necessary.

CONCLUSION

The first step in the marketing process is "WHAT DO YOU HAVE". The process of determining this needs to be done thoroughly and accurately, so that you know the people, goods, facts, services, and resources that surround you.

All of this knowledge will stand as a solid foundation as you proceed through the rest of the marketing process. You will find yourself referring to this information time and time again as you identify needs and work to establish exchange relationships.

This step is really the "homework" or "research" stage, put together from many parts and perspectives, and as such launches you toward success and truly "having your act together."

CHAPTER II — REFERENCES

1. Levitt, Theodore. *The Marketing Imagination,* The Free Press, 1983.
2. Kotler, Phillip. *Marketing for Nonprofit Organizations,* Prentice-Hall, 1975.
3. Levitt, Theodore. *The Marketing Imagination,* The Free Press, 1983.
4. Kotler, Phillip. *Marketing for Nonprofit Organizations,* Prentice-Hall, 1975.
5. Americans Volunteer. Gallup Poll, Independent Sector, 1983-84.
6. Scheier, Ivan. *Dovia Directory,* Yellow Fire Press, 1983.

7. Vineyard, Sue. *Finding Your Way Through The Maze of Volunteer Management,* Heritage Arts, 1981.

8. Americans Volunteer. Gallup Poll, Independent Sector, 1983-84.

9. Statistical Abstract, 1979.

10. Roscoe, Jerome. article: *Organizational Practioner,* July, 1979.

11. Ibid.

12. Statistical Abstract, 1979.

13. Roscoe, Jerome. article: *Organizational Practioner,* July, 1979.

14. Ibid.

15. Ibid.

16. Naisbitt, John. *Megatrends,* Warner Books, 1982.

CHAPTER III

Step Number 2: Knowing What You Need

"An uncreative mind can spot wrong answers;
it takes a creative mind to spot wrong questions."
... Marlene Wilson[1]

Whenever I introduce the four-step process in marketing, fundraising, planning, etc. I usually am greeted by strange looks when I mention "knowing what you need."

The various looks all add up to a "Well, of *course* we know what we need!," sent my direction with an odd "what's-*her*-problem?" look.

When, however, I ask people to specifically tell me what they need I get answers such as:

1. Volunteers

2. $10,000

3. More support

Sorry folks, but those answers do not tell me—or anyone—what you need. How many volunteers? To do what? When? For how long? What will the $10,000 be spent on? Who will benefit? What's the purpose? More support for what? When? How?

In expressing what is needed, discipline yourself to be as specific as possible so that those hearing the expressed needs have a clear understanding and can even picture what is required and *WHO WILL BENEFIT!*

In marketing, you can never move beyond the exercise of listing your publics and into the practical action of identifying which of these publics can become a potential market *unless* you know specifically what you need.

A cardinal rule of effective marketing is—it must be *targeted.* That simply means it is specifically aimed toward people or groups who can give you what you need. It seems obvious, then, that before targeting you must understand the need, specifically.

We can get into a real Catch 22 in an organization when specific needs are not expressed, and horror stories such as the following can emerge:

1. The Donor Department of the local Blood Bank calls the Volunteer Director, saying, "I need 20 volunteers the week of August 1st. They show up thinking they will assist donors and are horrified to find out they were needed to do clerical work. Three-fourths do not have the needed skills and one-fourth can't handle all the work. (By the way, the fault for this mess lies equally between the person who requested the volunteers without expressing the specific need for *clerical* workers, *and* the volunteer director who assumed, rather than checked, what they were needed for.)

2. A notice is put into the church paper and a pulpit plea is made during worship for volunteers to "help fix up the church on Saturday, August 10th at 9 A.M." August 10th dawns and 106 people show up asking, "What do you want me to do?" Unfortunately, there are only about fifteen job assignments. No one has made a list of other needs, secured enough tools, or appointed leadership. All day long work is found to "keep 'em busy" and, in fact, six people work hard all morning to move a pile of dirt from the front to the back of the church property, while five work just as hard all afternoon to return it to its original site!

3. A local women's club decides to hold a luncheon-fashion show and sets a goal of $5,000. During the ticket sales campaign the annual meeting of the club is held at which time it is revealed that they have $18,000 in the bank. This is reported in the local paper. People ask, "Where is the money from my ticket going?" and sellers reply, "I'm not sure . . . the general fund I guess." The ticket sales plunge.

Every one of those stories is drawn from real life, and every one is an example of either not knowing specifically what you need or, at the very least, not letting others know of those specifics.

CATEGORIES OF NEED

To be able to zero in on your needs, you may wish to think in terms of the categories of needs that exist.

With many sub-categories in each, they are:

1. People
2. Goods
3. Skills
4. Structure
5. Services
6. Cooperation and/or support
7. Dollars

PEOPLE

In looking at the need categories labeled "people," ask yourself:

1. How many people are needed?
2. To do what?
3. For how long? How many hours per week or month?
4. What special skills are required?
5. What energy level will be demanded of them?
6. Will they work as individuals or on a team?
7. What level of responsibility is required?
8. Are there opportunities for flex-space, flex-time or shared job assignments for these people?
9. What rewards might be available to them?

GOODS

In identifying tangible items needed for your volunteer program, determine:

1. What specifically is needed?
2. To do what?
3. For how long?
4. In what quantity?
5. Why is it needed?
6. Do you really need some item (i.e.: a computer) or do you only need what that item can do (computerization)? (The answer to this may switch your thinking from needing goods to needing a service.)

SKILLS

Some of the best time (and money) that can be spent on a volunteer program is that in which the director and key leaders/staff steal away to a refreshing mountain top or beach (a cool basement with no phones also works), and begin to sort out what their program really needs in terms of skills.

List all the jobs presently held, then all the dreams of jobs for the future. Next to each of these begin to list specific skills that are mandatory, desired, or needed. From these lists may emerge a pattern that reveals the need for such skills as a graphic artist, a computer programmer, people with pleasant phone personalities, and dozens of others.

You will leave your mountain/beach/basement armed with a much better understanding of specific skills needed throughout your organization—information that will spell more success in recruitment and placement later on. An added benefit is that retreat participants will have a clearer understanding of the skill needs of the *others,* making them able to share and recruit volunteers more effectively.

STRUCTURE

In determining needs of structure, it is critical to have a clear and honest idea of what structure presently exists in your organization and an assessment of just how much it can support.

A professional association that asked me to consult with them about a product they had developed but could not seem to "sell," revealed a good product, packaged poorly, with a weak delivery structure.

The people who had developed the product (a credentialing program) had assumed that the grassroots structure of the organization could take over on the massive promotion, training, organization, and mentoring required by the product. Unfortunately, the association was made up of relatively small numbers of individuals who did not know one another, had no formal structure other than a chairperson overseeing up to five states, and were routinely overworked in their own jobs.

My suggestion to get their product into a more "saleable" form was two-fold: 1) Simplify the process itself which was complex, discouraging, and impractical and, 2) Strengthen the local structure to facilitate delivery. (Recruit more people, train them, etc.)

"Structure" must be assessed carefully and regularly, examining:

1. What is already demanded of persent structure?
2. Where is it strongest? Weakest? (top/grassroots/middle, etc.)
3. What is needed to strengthen the structure?
4. What restraints influence the structure? (bylaws, standards, funding, management style of leaders, values, traditions, etc.)
5. Are there clear job designs? Goals and objectives? Timelines?
6. Are there paid staff or volunteers or a mixture of both?
7. Is the structure set up to initiate action or simply respond to events?
8. Where/who are the power sources and decision makers?
9. How rigid/flexible is the structure?

A good organizational chart is needed for an overview of the structure plus a healthy dose of realism about how effectively it presently works. The conclusion of this assessment will reveal whether your structure is weak or strong. This will be invaluable information for marketing as it will tell you where you need to shore it up, avoid it, or use its rich potential.

SUPPORT/COOPERATION

When you begin to specifically assess needs, do not overlook the critical importance of the support you require to carry out your work. Too frequently, people omit this less tangible factor in their needs assessment and then can't figure out later why they are not having success.

In marketing planning one support that is needed is a TOTAL ORGANIZATION MARKETING PERSPECTIVE. Admittedly, most volunteer programs exist in a climate that may *not* recognize marketing as necessary (remember, marketing is relatively new to non-profit's thinking.) I encourage you, however, to work toward influencing the organization to such a marketing perspective.

When in place this perspective will offer:

1. Clear direction from the top on goals, etc.
2. Control and coordination from the top on all the marketing aspects going on in the organization at once.
3. Continuity of marketing efforts.
4. Involvement in the decision-making process by people, such as yourself, who must plan and implement marketing strategies.
5. A willingness to act and change strategies as needed.
6. Plans and budgets in line with mission.
7. Periodic review of marketing efforts.

If influencing the whole organization seems too formidable a task, I suggest you acquire permission to use a marketing approach in your volunteer services department. Not only will your department benefit, it can hopefully stand as an example for the rest of the organization to follow.

DOLLARS

In assessing what funding you will need, be careful to break figures down into bite-sized, tangible bits. One of the most frequent reasons for people being turned down when they request funds is that they never cause the potential donor to have any emotional or personalized attachment to a cold-sounding dollar figure.

The trick in getting people or groups to donate money is to help them envision the *results* of their donation in "people-helped" terms.

The total figure is simply an accountant's reference and says nothing about effectiveness, helping people specifically, making a difference, etc. etc.

Look at any budget figures you have, assessing how those dollars would be spent:

1. What things purchased? (wheelchairs, computer, van, etc.)
2. Who would be helped by these things?
3. What services would these funds purchase? (clerical, theraputic, managerial, etc.)
4. How will the agency clients be helped by these services? (better records, skill building, stronger organization, etc.)

In brainstorming the specific needs funding might meet, you may begin to come up with a catalog of needs that can be advertised to potential donors. It has been found to be easier to get an individual or group to donate a wheelchair (cost $500) to a program than to get the same group to simply give you a $500 donation. The wheelchair is tangible and instantly implies helping a person. The check is impersonal and intangible in people's minds and may cause some more cynical members of a group to wonder if it won't go to recarpet an executive's office!

MANAGEMENT—THE TOOL
REQUIRED TO MAP PROGRAM NEEDS

The tool of management is critical in all phases of marketing, as you organize your efforts, assess needs, implement strategies, etc. It helps you "get your act together" (the 11th Commandment!) in order that you can be successful.

As groups ask me to consult with them on problems, I find that in 9 out of 10 cases, the root problem was the lack of understanding of management, causing parts of the process to be out of order or omitted completely.

To help people understand the management process, its functions, components, and sequence, I devised the visual of a bridge that follows.

FIRST—THE DREAM

Carl Sandburg said, "Nothing happens, but first a dream." As you look at the bridge please note that it begins on a block labeled "DREAM" and ends on a block labeled "REALITY."

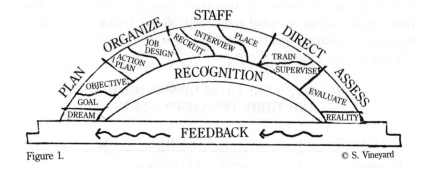

Figure 1.   © S. Vineyard

Management is the bridge, or structure, which can turn our dreams into reality if built carefully and properly. This whole concept of building a bridge is dependent on people being able to dream, envision reality, and take the necessary steps to bridge the gap between the two. In short, it takes a *leader.*

Mike Murray, a fellow trainer whom I hold in highest regard, defines a leader as a person who has dreams and visions and can cause others to catch sight of those dreams and visions *in such a way that they want to invest themselves and become part of the process.*

Another insight into the importance of envisioning lies in a recent study by psychologist Charles Garfield of what makes people successful. His work[2] lists six characteristics of successful people from all areas of life.

Successful People:

1. Work for the art of it.

2. Set own, higher, compelling goals.

3. Don't blame—problem solve.

4. Take the risks after laying out the worst consequences beforehand.

5. CAN ENVISION RESULTS AND REHEARSE ACTIONS MENTALLY.

6. Avoid so called "comfort zones."

BUILDING YOUR BRIDGE . . .

After the dreams have been formed, communicated to others, and their reality envisioned, the management bridge can be built. Nothing

62

is more critical to your marketing plans than your ability to manage your efforts. To understand more fully all the various parts of the process, I encourage you to read Marlene Wilson's book, *The Effective Management of Volunteer Programs*[3]

THE FIVE FUNCTIONS OF MANAGEMENT
AND THEIR TEN COMPONENTS

FUNCTION	COMPONENTS
1. Planning	1. Goal, 2. Objectives,
2. Organizing	3. Plans of action, 4. Job design,
3. Staffing	5. Recruit, 6. Interview, 7. Place,
4. Directing	8. Train, 9. Supervise,
5. Assessing	10. Evaluate

Let's define each:

THE PLANNING FUNCTION—

Component #1. *Goal*—The mission statement: tells what you want to do for either your whole volunteer program or any small part of it (recruitment, recognition banquet, etc.).

Component #2. *Objectives*—Statements of direction that begin to break this goal down into bite sized and manageable pieces. They start with the word "to," implying needed action, and are *specific, measurable, achievable,* and *compatible* with the overall mission. There will be several objectives for the one goal.

THE ORGANIZING FUNCTION—

Component #3. *Plans of Action*—Statements that tell *who* will do what, *when* they will do it, a sketch of *how* they will do it, and what that action will *cost* in time, energy, and/or dollars.

Let's stop and look at an example of how these three components flow together to help you understand your needs:

Goal: To enlarge the volunteer staff of the hospital.

Objectives: #1— To recruit 50 more volunteers by January 1st of next year (8 months away) to work in the new out-patient program.

#2— To form a Speakers Bureau of five volunteers by September 1st (3 months away) trained to talk to local service groups and churches about the program and recruit new volunteers.

#3— To secure a volunteer to produce a color/sound slide show on the volunteer program by September 1st to be used by the Speakers Bureau.

Plans of Action for Objective #2

A. To *form* the Speakers Bureau:

Who: Asst. Dir. of Volunteers

When: April - Sept.

How: Identify present volunteers with public speaking skills, experience, and group contacts (information in your resource file)

Cost: $: staff time; time: two hours per week

B. For the people who *are on* the Speakers Bureau:

Who: Key volunteer leaders

When: Sept. - June (training in August)

How: Contact group leaders, schedule presentations, delivery followup on interested people.

Cost: $: Gas reimbursement; Time: one meeting per month for each; Training: three hours on August 31st.

Component #4: *Job Design:* For each plan of action one or more job designs will be required. The points that need to be covered in a job design (Please note the intentional use of the word "design" rather than "description." This is to indicate flexibility rather than rigidity.) are:

a. *Title*—Truth in packing please! Let it say what it is.

b. *Responsible for*—What is to be done?

c. *Responsible to*—Who supervises them?

   d. *Skills*—Any special abilities needed?

   e. *Time:*—How long do they have to do it? What time will it require by day/week/month etc.?

   f. *Parameters*—Any factors that will influence the work, such as training provided, materials and support, past history, how work is to be evaluated, any governing policies, etc. etc.

To follow the example one step further, the job design for plan of action "B" above (referring to people who are to be on the Speakers Bureau):

Title: SPEAKER

Responsible for:
1. Attend training August 31, 9 A.M. to 12 noon
2. Contacting local groups assigned, to secure invitation to address groups, encourage support and recruit volunteers.
3. Report interest to recruitment chair, in writing.

Responsible to:
Chair, Speakers Bureau

Time:
1. Training: August 31, 9 A.M. to 12 noon.
2. Speaking: one group per month, Sept.—Jan. 1st, 1-2 hours per group and reporting time

Skills:
1. Public speaking
2. Knowledge of program

Parameters:
1. Training will explain key points, how to sign up volunteers, how to report, sharpening speaking skills, use of slide show, etc.
2. Support—Consultation with chair and/or Director of Volunteers, information on groups from Resource File, 12 minute sound/color slide show on program, speaking outline, follow-up by Recruitment Chair.

3. History—there has been no such formalized approach to groups in the past.

4. How evaluated—January - Speakers Bureau meeting to assess success, opportunities for growth, etc.

5. Policies—
   a. no speaker may promise any specific assignment to any group or individual.
   b. personnel matters are never discussed
   c. confidentiality on patient's information is kept at all times.

THE STAFFING FUNCTION—

Component #5: *Recruit:* This component brings us full circle to marketing, since recruiting is simply a form of marketing—getting who you need in exchange for returned values to the recruit. Another name for recruitment is "enlistment" or the signing on of people to do specific jobs.

A WORD HERE REGARDING RECRUITMENT "NO—NO's!"

The approach to recruitment is critical. Considering the fact that so many people continue to use poor recruitment methods it's a wonder we have as many volunteers as we do! Do you recognize any of the following "no-no's as ones you've seen used or—worse yet—ones you've had used on you?

NO-NO #1—*"There's nothing TO IT" method*—tries to convince people the job is easy, simple and "no sweat." Count on it being hard, complex, and frought with danger. These are usually "BIG SWEAT" jobs!

NO-NO #2—*"First Warm Body Through the Door" method*—this indicates greater concern for filling a slot than matching people's needs and skills to jobs that require or offer those same characteristics. Following such recruitment tactics you find a lot of questions, such as "How come someone who can't speak English is assigned to talk to the Retired Teachers Association?" or, "Why is the janitor on every committee?" or, "Why was Martha asked to cut her 100th birthday party short to coach the track team?"

NO-NO #3—*"Buffalo Bill" method*—the process adapted from buffalo hunters whereby you wait till one silly buffalo gets separated from the herd and can be trapped. The translation to volunteerism is that some recruiters will wait until a person is absent from a meeting to "appoint" them to a position. One of my workshop participants shared that this was the traditional way Circle chairs were "chosen" at her church, and that the groups had to use the church auditorium to accommodate all the people who came to the meeting where next year's chair was appointed!

Any of the above negative methods of recruitment are in reality, the *opposite* of the real definitions of marketing, for they not only omit the factor of the trade of value for value, they really have *no* value. Inappropriate, unhappy people are "stuck" with jobs they are not equipped to handle.

As you delegate recruitment responsibilities to others, insure that negative methods are avoided and the basics of good value-exchange marketing are embraced.

The danger of such inappropriate recruitment is that dissatisfied, poorly placed volunteers share their dissatisfaction with others. The best recruiters available to you are satisfied volunteers who tell others about their work, encouraging participation and commitment (these are AGENT publics) and appropriate recruitment is the greatest tool to encourage this positive fallout.

Component #6: *Interview:* An interview is defined by Marlene Wilson[4] as a "conversation with a purpose" and is the vehicle of communication which allows a prospective volunteer and the volunteer director to know more about service opportunities in the organization *and* to uncover the skills, needs, motivations, and experiences of the volunteer. In this initial conversation the effective interviewer uses the art of indirect questioning to assess potential value trades between the agency and the individual. Four types of interviews continue to assess value exchanges:

1) the screening interview, 2) the placement interview, 3) the on-the-job interview and 4) the exit interview.

Component #7:   *Place:* This component is the actual matching of the person to the job and moves the management process from preliminary work of finding potential people for appropriate jobs into the action part of making dreams come true. This placement component is critical to the eventual success of the dream. Too frequently people attribute failures to "wrong people in jobs." This is not accurate, but rather *right* people were in wrong jobs. This puts the focus back on the person placing the volunteer, rather than dumping blame on an inappropriately placed recruit.

THE DIRECTING FUNCTION . . .

Component #8:   *Training:* After being placed in a job, volunteers must be trained and equipped to enable their success. As you assess needs in your program, the plans for training are critical and will demand attention to well equipped trainers, good materials, appropriate site and environment, and effective tools.

Component #9:   *Supervise:* The singularly most important component in the management process is the supervision of staff, either paid or non-paid. To simplify the choices of management styles (there are many variations) remember that there are really only two ways to supervise—you can ENABLE or you can DISABLE people you direct. The disabler will not delegate honestly, does not trust subordinates, withholds information, feels the only "good" project is one they do themselves, does not recognize efforts positively, is rigid and/or refuses to lend assistance. The ENABLER, in addition to the *opposite* of all of the above characteristics, expends energies in the art of growing people to their potential so

68

that they can enjoy the success of the dream's reality along with the agency.

THE ASSESSING FUNCTION . . .

Component #10: *Evaluate:* The final component in the management process is the evaluation of efforts. Success is compared to the original goal and objectives, and the ultimate "feelings" surrounding the effort. In assessing marketing efforts, you will measure desired results against accomplishments. Be careful, however, to avoid the pitfall of too narrow an assessment having only to do with numbers. In our field, feelings and reputation are important and can influence future success greatly. In fundraising, for instance, groups often only assess results by how much money was earned rather than any added values coming from greater PR and visability, more volunteers involved with the cause and/or new program ideas that will serve the agency in the long range. The critical factors for positive evaluation are:

a. Involve as many points of view as possible.

b. Focus on issues, not personalities

c. Applaud success.

d. Identify opportunities for greater success (vs. identifying "failures").

e. Never give "negative-you" messages. (i.e.: "You really loused that up!")

f. Avoid "shoulds" and "oughts" that make people feel guilty and inadequate.

g. Keep any necessary attention to individual negative efforts private and confidential.

Several years ago I came in contact with a group that had, the year before, put on a fundraiser that had made $67,000. Encouraged by that success, the group decided to repeat their effort the following year, setting the goal at $100,000. They then relayed this goal to the charities' out of state C.E.O.

Unfortunately their community was a "one-industry" town, and that one industry called a wildcat strike one month prior to the event. Rather than throwing in the towel, however, in what appeared to be a bleak financial climate, the event committee rolled up their sleeves, and came up with dozens of creative "friendraising" ideas to increase revenues.

Radio stations, industry management and labor, school children, local businesses etc. all were involved, with the incredible result that $97,000 was raised!

To celebrate this success, a "Love-In" was planned at a local high school gym. Volunteers were asked to bring casseroles to share plus several people who had helped them in their volunteer effort. As a result parents brought kids who had put up with quickie dinners, people brought neighbors who had loaned materials or babysitting chores, etc. etc.

Sadly, one other person came, armed with a letter to all the volunteers—the charities' C.E.O., who had been so charming when the planning committee had shared their $100,000 goal months before.

How horrified everyone was as they read the C.E.O.'s letter, which began: "How dare you come to within $3,000 of your goal and fall short! Now I have to go to the Board and report that if only the people of ———— had worked a little harder they could have had a success!

This is a horror story to be sure, but a classic example of how evaluation can be used negatively and can *disable* people.

THE BRIDGE COMPLETED . . . TWO MORE FACTORS . . .

With the five management functions and their ten components in order, properly sequenced and with none omitted, the process is complete. The success of your effort will *not* be complete, however, without two additional factors:

1. RECOGNITION

2. FEEDBACK AND COMMUNICATION

RECOGNITION

The buttress of the entire bridge is *appropriate* recognition that undergirds all of the components so that people involved feel good about their experience. In examining needs, do not overlook this vital factor. Keep in mind that good recognition is:[5]

1. *User* oriented
2. Appropriate to the effort (avoiding over or under recognizing)
3. Involving people in decisions that affect them
4. More *informal* than formal
5. Often be expressed through fun and humor
6. Immediate
7. Varied, flexible, and creative
8. Visible to others as well as the recipient

FEEDBACK AND COMMUNICATION

The foundation on which the bridge rests is the communication channel through which flows the information and assessments of the effort.

This feedback stimulates new dreams and influences future planning, organizing, staffing, directing, and assessing. Whenever you can learn from your experiences, through open communication flow, you potentially strengthen your future efforts.

In marketing, this flow, from as many perspectives as possible, is the key to future success in the trade of value for value and the "selling" of your volunteer program.

THE NEED FOR MARKETING INTELLIGENCE

Several pieces of knowledge are required as you plan your marketing exchanges. They include:

1. The need to separate "needs" and "wants" in your mind. They are *very* different and, if undefined, can clutter priority setting.
2. Research conducted periodically of key target markets.
3. Competitions efforts regularly tracked and analyzed.
4. Long-range strategic issues identified to guide annual planning.
5. Regular evaluation of organization and program effectiveness versus objectives, efficiency etc.

6. Relevant quality information is regularly available in a form useful for decision making. (NO MUMBO-JUMBO!)

Together, these items comprise a program's "marketing intelligence." If any of them are missing, work to get them reinstated. I have seen groups strategize their marketing plans totally inappropriately because of false or incomplete information.

THE FINAL NEED

That is a rather ominous heading to close this chapter, but indeed there is one more, somewhat incalculable need you will have as a volunteer administrator embarking into the world of marketing.

That final requirement is an attitudinal one, a passion if you will, for the dream you have in mind. The more complex or lofty the dream, the more energy, organization, strategizing, and creativity it will require. You will personally need a *passionate faith* in your dream's outcome, its value to all concerned, and its effectiveness in human services.

The dream is the destination; the process is the marketing; the vehicle is management, but the fuel is passion!

CONCLUSION

Step two of the marketing process, WHAT DO YOU NEED, must be assessed and described specifically from many angles: physical, emotional, personnel, supportive, and financial to name a few.

When, indeed, you have looked at these categories and others you deem appropriate to your goals, you will have the first part of the exchange relationship well defined as you identify what is needed, and therefore its VALUE, to your program.

The next two steps put the second part of the relationship into focus as you identify values to potential volunteers, donors, etc. and move on to the exchange of these values to the satisfaction of both parties.

CHAPTER III — REFERENCES

1. Marlene Wilson, *How to Mobilize Volunteers in the Church,* Augsburg Press, 1983.

2. Charles Garfield, "Why Do Some People Outperform Others? *Wall Street Journal,* January 1982.

3. Marlene Wilson, *The Effective Management of Volunteer Programs,* Volunteer Management Associates, Boulder, Colorado, 1976.

4. Ibid.

5. Sue Vineyard, *Beyond Banquets, Plaques and Pins: Creative Ways to Recognize Volunteers and Staff,* Heritage Arts Publishers, Downers Grove, Illinois, 1982.

CHAPTER IV

Step Number 3: Who Has What You Need?

"Everything the organization does or proclaims must be tailored to the consumer's needs: What the service accomplishes, how it is packaged, how it is sold, and when and where it is presented."
. . . Paul Wagner[7]

The third step toward success is marketing your volunteer program is to identify and discover which individuals, groups, sectors, etc. have what you need.

In step #1 you mapped out potential resources called publics. In step #2 you identified the specific needs your program has in the way of people, goods, services, dollars, or support.

At this point, you are ready to move on to the matching of resources and needs, and to locate, from your publics, those individuals and groups who can meet your needs.

This step brings you to the second component of marketing which is the MARKET itself. Remember that a *MARKET* is defined as an identified public with whom you decide you wish to have a trade relationship. To put it more simply: *THEY HAVE WHAT YOU WANT OR NEED!*

HOW A PUBLIC BECOMES A MARKET . . .

As you look at your publics chart, with its hundreds of identified groups and classifications, you should be able to see those that could provide a specific need.

An example might be:

NEED: 25 volunteers to staff the annual health fair on Sat. Oct. 1st at the local high school.

PUBLICS THAT COULD BECOME MARKETS:

a. Local Jr. Women's Club (Health Committee)

b. Kiwanis Club

c. St. Mark's Lutheran Church

d. Future Nurse's Assn.

e. Pre-retirement Club (at local business)

(There would be dozens of others, but prioritization may have placed these five at the top of your list. Also, you would have job designs to know length of shifts, skills needed, etc.)

As you zero in on publics that could meet your need, you are changing their definition to a MARKET—targeted and potentially a partner in a value exchange. Be very cautious at this point *not* to make decisions for that public. This is one of the most restricting, yet frequently made, errors possible—that of saying "no" for someone else.

When this attitude of negative pre-judging other's reaction takes over in a group, true brainstorming is squelched and many potentially successful relationships are killed before they are even given a chance.

Keep a positive attitude. It is possible that past "nos" from a person or group may have been a result of the wrong asking technique, or more frequently—asking the wrong person for the wrong thing at the wrong time. Keep previous "nos" in the past where they belong and be positive about future "yesses." *Every good salesperson knows it takes seven "nos" before a "yes" comes along!*

THE MARKETING PLAN—Part One:
Analysis and Prioritization

As you identify a need and groups that could provide the answer to that need, you have actually begun to formulate a marketing plan which maps out:

1. The specific need

2. Potential markets

3. Contacts within the markets

4. What value your group could offer in an exchange

5. Who would be the right person to contact within the market and who should make the contact.

6. Information regarding the market

In chart form this looks like:

NEED	(MARKET) WHO HAS?	INSIDE CONTACT(S)	WHAT VALUE CAN WE TRADE?	GENERAL INFORMATION (WHO? WHEN? HISTORY? STRATEGY? ETC.)
25 vols. for Health Fair, Sat. Oct. 1	1. Jr. Women's	1. Sue Smith (555-1111) is V.P. 2. John Jones (555-6210) wife is member	1. good publicity 2. fulfill requirements of health comm. award 3. meet purpose of service to community	1. meet in H.S. 4th Tues./ mo. 8 p.m. 2. Pres.: Kay Wylie (555-3596) 3. HELPED FAIR: 1967-1973 4. Need to present to Health Comm. (Jan. Jones, Chr.) 5. No club calendar 6. Sue Smith best contact
	2. Future Nurse's Assn.	1. Peg Ross's daughter, Pres.	1. Fulfill hrs. of service demand 2. Could get Nat'l attention 3. Good PR 4. Credit for resume	1. 26 membership meet 4th Fri. in H.S. 2. Mrs. Marker is adviser (PE teacher) 3. Looking for practical work 4. Peg R. best contact along with daughter Susan

3. Pre-retirement club at (local bus.)	1. Jeff Mitchell very active in club	1. Worthwhile service	1. Looking for worthwhile service
	2. Barb Miller's brother & sister-in-law active	2. Good PR	2. Company wanting to ease people into volunteering
			3. Best contact: Jeff Mitchell

As you go through this process, you are actually analyzing each potential market—looking at its strengths and weaknesses along with the various factors that will help you decide *which* market to approach first. The rule of thumb in determining this is: GO WITH THE MARKET THAT AFFORDS THE STRONGEST CHANCE FOR A SUCCESSFUL RELATIONSHIP.

In my thinking, this works out to be the market TO WHOM YOU CAN OFFER THE GREATEST AMOUNT OF VALUE. In other words—you are offering at *least* as much, if not more, than you are asking.

Please note that the bulk of the information has come from the Resource Inventory File you put together in step #1 (What Do You Have?). As you can see, the more information gathered regarding a group in the form of contacts, purpose, meeting data, etc. the more you have to work with as you prepare your strategy.

The strategizing that comes after this first step toward a marketing plan will be more fully discussed in chapter #4 (HOW DO YOU GET WHAT YOU NEED?).

THE DIFFERENCE BETWEEN "NEEDS" AND "WANTS" . . .

A word of caution here as you map out your efforts in behalf of your program. I find that people often confuse "needs" and "wants," and thus diffuse their energies.

A "need" is a mandatory article or person; a "want" is desired but non-mandatory. You *need* 25 volunteers to staff the Health Fair because you have promised them to the fair organizers. You might also *want* an extra 25 to cut the two-hour shifts down to one, but you can survive without them.

In this age where so many groups are rushing for computers, I find some groups who really *do* "need" a computer (to sort through mountains of files, volunteer records, etc.) and others who *want* a computer but could get along without one. BE CAREFUL TO DISTINGUISH BETWEEN NEEDS AND WANTS . . . putting your primary energies into meeting your *needs!*

AN EXERCISE TO IDENTIFY MARKETS

1. Gather a group of key people from your program.

2. List your major needs on a blackboard.

3. Determine the priority of these needs.

4. Taking one need at a time, and using your Publics Chart and Resource File, create a Marketing Chart as shown in this chapter.

5. Discuss the market's priority—who you will go to first, when, how, etc.

6. Map out plans of action.

MOTIVATION . . . A Key Tool of Success

"There's no great trick to motivation.
It's simply finding out what people like to do
and can do well, and then letting them do it!"
. . . Peter Drucker

In working to establish a fulfilling trade relationship with others, *and* to keep that relationship strong as you work together, another of the four key tools becomes a necessity for the effective volunteer administrator.

The tool is that of MOTIVATION—its basic understanding and how to utilize it in daily efforts.

It is not necessary to have advanced degrees in behavioral science or psychology to grasp and use the learning that comes from these sciences. It is however, vitally important that you have a common sense handle on several different theories in order to better understand why people do what they do.

MOTIVATION—What It Is and How To Measure It

Good old Webster's (New World Dictionary, Student Edition, Prentice Hall) says that "motive" means "some inner drive, impulse etc. that causes one to act in a certain way" and that motivation means "to be impelled by a motive."

To put it into even more graphic terms, motivation seems to mean hitting someone's "hot" button (and avoiding their "turn-off" button!)

In working to train audiences in motivation, I ask participants to name things they love to do. I jot these on a blackboard and usually end up with a list that includes:

—Working with kids
—Doing research
—Playing tennis
—Reading
—Compiling statistics
—Public speaking
—Working on a task force
—Working alone etc. etc. etc.

It's always interesting to watch facial expressions in the group as things are called out. The person sharing the thing they like to do almost always has a pleased and satisfied look on their face, and is joined by others who obviously also like to do that same thing and show it by nodding their head, smiling and saying, "Oh, yes!" or "Me, too!"

The contrast comes from the facial expressions on some of the other participants who register a "you've-got-to-be-kidding" look along with an occasional exclamation, such as, "Yuck!" Obviously, these people are reacting to someone elses joy as their "junk"!

When we talk about the fact that what turns some people "on" turns others "off," we have the beginning of an understanding of how motivations can vary from person to person and job to job.

This is highly valuable information and helps you understand:

1. The differences between varied motivations

2. That not everyone shares *your* motivations

80

3. That identification of different motivations among your key leadership can offer different views of the same effort, personnel, plans, etc.

4. Why different people are attracted to different roles.

THEORIES OF MOTIVATION/NEED etc.

There are several theories and studies dealing with motivations, needs, satisfactions, expectations, and success. We'll examine each briefly, suggesting implications for volunteer programs. I encourage you to read more on each, and I have included reference information to lead you to further study.

MASLOW'S HIERARCHY OF NEEDS . . .

Many of you, after reading the above sub-heading, may want to skip this section, thinking you will become ill if you have to read about Maslow's hierarchy one more time. PLEASE DON'T SKIP OVER THIS! In spite of many debates on Old Abe's work, I think we can learn from the basics he lays out. The more understanding we have of the people who potentially will become partners in desired exchange relationships, the more "handles" we can have in establishing and maintaining those relationships.

Maslow's Hierarchy of Needs [1] offers insight into five levels of need he documented in human beings. It admittedly does not take into account spiritual needs, but it was not intended to do so when it was devised.

The five levels of need are:

Level #1 Physiological (food, water, air, etc.)

Level #2 Safety (shelter, defense, etc.)

Level #3 Social (friends, relationships, etc.)

Level #4 Esteem (to be valued, admired, etc.)

Level #5 Self-Actualization (to reach your potential, to develop talents)

Maslow diagramed his theory of needs in the form of a triangle, with level #1 being at the bottom, level #5 at the top. This serves to illustrate that most people in the world exist at the lower levels of need, having to put their energies into providing food and shelter for themselves.

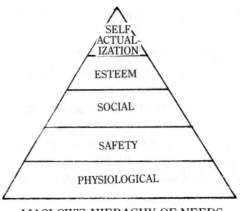

Figure 1.   MASLOW'S HIERACHY OF NEEDS

Maslow made several key points regarding his needs theory. These are critical points to keep in mind as we assess volunteer's motivations.

1. *UN-MET NEEDS MOTIVATE:* When a person senses an un-met need, they will respond to opportunities to meet this need. Examples:

   a. When people feel they have *un*used gifts they will often welcome opportunities to use those gifts in volunteer placements. (self-actualization)

   b. When people feel unrecognized, undervalued, or anonymous elsewhere, they may seek opportunities to be rewarded, openly recognized, and spotlighted through outstanding volunteer efforts. (esteem)

   c. When people feel lonely, they may seek volunteer opportunities that will allow them to meet and mix with other people. (socialization)

   d. People who are fearful of losing their jobs, will often welcome chances to build skills, gain new experiences or expand their resumes through volunteer work. (safety)

   e. People who have fixed or lower incomes may deeply appreciate and desire volunteer opportunities that happen to have a free meal attached to them or offer them a winter-heated or summer-cooled site in which to work, so they can remain comfortable *without* expending their own energy dollars. (physiological)

82

In each of the examples above—the stimulation for action is an *un-met* need.

2. *PEOPLE ARE MOTIVATED BY THE LOWEST LEVEL OF UN-MET NEED:* If you have people who are really "into" self-actualization working in your office, take note that their flurry of activity (creating, devising, refining, etc.) begins to ebb as meal time approaches. This is because the need for food (physiological) becomes stronger than the need to self-actualize. The same is true about fatigue—the need for rest becomes greater than any higher level needs at the end of a day.

This lesson was really brought home to me while I was National Director of Project Concern International. I had one of my key people, who normally was motivated by self-actualization, confound me one day. She had been working for several months on a proposal for a new program to serve our agency and was to present it at an upcoming national meeting.

When I inquired as to how it was going (the meeting was a week away), she seemed disinterested saying, "Oh, I uh, haven't thought much about it. I don't even know if I can go to the meeting."

A gentle probe, and a suspicion that there had to be more to the story, revealed that her doctor had discovered a problem in a regular medical check-up, and she was scheduled for a biopsy in a few days.

What had happened was that her attention, energies, etc. were being motivated by safety concerns for her health. Her "normal" self-actualization need had been pre-empted! After the biopsy proved no need for worry, she immediately bounced back to her natural stance.

3. *MET NEEDS NO LONGER MOTIVATE*—Often in our field, we refer to people who have "burned out" in a job or those who we judge as no longer "effective." A deeper examination often reveals people who were placed in a job that met their needs at the time but whose needs have changed.

When my boys were one and three and my husband Wes and I were quite new to Downers Grove, I felt a deep need for new friends, adult companionship, and some conversation that reached beyond the confines of Captain Kangaroo and nursery rhymes! All of these needs (of socialization) were met when I joined the local Junior Women's

Club, meeting many new people and establishing numerous life-long relationships. The first job I took as a volunteer with them was that of being on the Social Committee because it afforded me so many opportunities to meet new people.

After about nine months, however, our calendar seemed to have no blank spots and making more new friends no longer became a prime motivation.

My socialization need had been met and no longer stimulated me. Fortunately, I was able to move on to satisfy a new need, but I've often wondered how long I would have remained enthusiastic had I been forced to stay on the Social Committee.

Sadly, I hear from many people who feel they are "stuck" in a volunteer job long after it loses interest for them. They are the first to admit they are no longer doing a "good job." I would guess people around them are attributing their work level to "burnout." The truth is the person has not "burned out" at all; they simply are inappropriately placed in a job.

4. *PEOPLE ARE CONSTANTLY CHANGING AND EVEN COMBINING NEED LEVELS:* Labeling people by Maslow's hierarchy could be a dangerous sport and highly misleading. People move up and down the triangle daily and have different needs in different segments of their lives. I doubt that anyone could remain at the "self-actualization" level 100% of the time. Let's face it, sleeping and eating do have to interject themselves occasionally along with praise, relationships, and security!

In marketing, Maslow's teachings can prove an invaluable tool to help us assess appropriate value (or need) trades between people and agencies.

McCLELLAND'S MOTIVATIONAL CLASSIFICATIONS

David McClelland, a noted psychologist, conducted a fascinating study[2] of what motivates people, and then grouped these motivations under three classifications: AFFILIATION, ACHIEVEMENT, and POWER.

Much like the warning tag on pillows that threatens instant reprisal should you ever remove it, let me add a warning about the three classifications: PEOPLE ARE NEVER JUST ONE TYPE, BUT A DYNAMIC MIXTURE OF ALL THREE.

I always have a fear, after introducing McClelland's work to trainees, that they might go out and begin to brand people as one or the other, never bothering to check back to see about any changes!

There are several "givens" that must be understood as we look at McClelland's research:

1. *PEOPLE WANT TO BE SUCCESSFUL:* Only a very few, and very *strange,* people set out to be unsuccessful. (Actually their failure *is* their success—they are caught in a "I'm-no-good-watch-and-see-me-fail" syndrome). The tie-in between people's motivation and success is that they want their energies to go toward successful outcomes and those energies are best stimulated by what motivates or "turns them on."

2. *PEOPLE HAVE ALL THREE MOTIVATIONS, BUT ONE DOMINATES THE OTHER TWO:* Like cream that rises to the top of a milk bottle (did that just date me?), one motivation becomes stronger than the others in various situations.

   a. At various times in your life, different motivations will dominate. In early years affiliation motivations are strong; in middle years achievement or power motivations can be dominant, and in later years there is often a return to affiliation needs.

   b. In different segments of your life, you can have different motivations. When I am training I am motivated by an intense desire to influence and impact people's lives so that they can be more effective in working with volunteers (power or empowerment motivation). When I am in my role as vice-president of the Association For Volunteer Administration, I am trying to set and accomplish organizational goals (achievement). When I have the joy of spending time with family and friends I am simply enjoying those relationships (affiliation). All this is going on at the same time, and I slip from one to the other instantly.

Let's look at a diagram of McClelland's theory and define the three classifications.

1. *Affiliation:* the need to have relationships, to interact with others, to be liked and accepted, to work on teams and task forces. People with this primary motivation respond best to marketing requests that allow them to interact with clients and

other volunteers and to build personal relationships with supervisors and peers. They spend time thinking about how everyone "feels" as they work; they worry about hurt feelings and work to include everyone. They avoid conflicts and want people to be happy. They love committees, social gatherings, meetings in people's homes, receptionist and hosting jobs, etc.

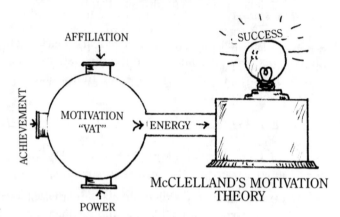

Figure 2.

2. *Achievement:* the need to set goals and accomplish those goals. People motivated by achievement think in terms of numbers and concrete ways of measuring success. They love lists and love to check things off of lists. They are often analytical, require direct regular feedback to measure success, want results documented, love a challenge, and need to know any groundrules or parameters in advance. Frequently they jump at opportunities to fundraise, lead a project, design strategies, plan events, analyze statistics, and keep records. They do not have an overriding need to work with others, and in fact, work perfectly happily by themselves, as long as they have regular feedback from their supervisor on progress.

3. *Power:* as Marlene Wilson states, "Power is *not* a four-letter word." Power, in the sense that McClelland uses it, simply means to influence and impact others. In an expansion of his definition of power, McClelland differentiates between positive (for the good of the group, enabling, empowerment, shared/combined strength) and negative (personalized, manipulative, coercive, punative, "me-first") power. People who are motivated by positive power love to be told something cannot be done, as

they love the challenge that lays before them. They usually form and articulate strong opinions, and respond to well-titled positions that leave no doubt as to their authority. They enjoy challenging authority, making changes, creating new ways to accomplish goals, and leading widely-based efforts. Jobs that can be marketed to them successfully may include chairperson of the board, lead donor in a fundraising campaign, advocate, public speaker, ombudsman, campaign director, etc.

In looking at McClelland's work, we can learn much about people and volunteer opportunities and where the motivations of each might be matched. Just as people display specific motivations, so also do various volunteer opportunities.

AN EXERCISE IN CLASSIFYING WORK

1. List the jobs your program offers to volunteers.

2. Classify each by McClelland's motivational classifications.

3. Note those jobs that hold more than one classification potential, depending on how they are carried out.

4. List specific needs of your programs (a computer, support for a project, etc.) and brainstorm what motivation each could bring out in an individual or group who might meet that need (i.e.: need for computer might be met by donation of software company needing a tax break, good publicity and advertisement for their software products.)

HERZBERG'S "MOTIVATION-HYGIENE" THEORY—

Another perspective that can help you identify who has what you need, comes from Fredrick Herzberg's studies[3] on motivation in work.

In establishing and maintaining the value exchanges your work requires, it is critical for you to understand that aspects surrounding work efforts are important to the success of future marketing.

Because your marketing "agents" are satisfied volunteers, and because the promise of satisfying work is the best recruitment tool, attention needs to be given to Herzberg's theory which separates "hygiene factors" and "MOTIVATORS."

Herzberg tells us that:

1. *Hygiene Factors* such as working conditions, rules, etc. do not in themselves motivate people, but *absence* of same will de-motivate. In other words, volunteers will probably take the proper building temperature at your work site for granted, rarely thanking you for it, but if the air is too cold, they will try to get the heat turned up, take time discussing the problem with peers, and possibly leave their work because of it. (If you want to test Herzberg's theory, park in someone else's parking space tomorrow and see how much diversion from assigned work it causes!)

2. *Motivators* are factors that stimulate people to action, causing them to remain satisfied in their work. When they are not present, people expend energies in frustration, becoming dissatisfied and reducing the quality of work.

Herzberg's theory can be diagrammed:

HYGIENE FACTORS	MOTIVATORS
Rules	1. Sense of achievement
Structure	2. Challenging work
Physical surroundings	3. Recognition for
Policies	accomplishments
Benefits	4. Increased
Work location	responsibility
Parking spaces	5. Personal growth and
Ease of building access	development
etc. etc.	

As you examine the work you are asking volunteers to do, look at the five factors of motivation to see how many are present in that work. You will have greater success in marketing when the work is perceived as motivating.

VROOM'S THEORY OF EXPECTANCY

One last theory related to motivation and work efforts is worth noting here . . . Victor Vroom's[4] intricate theory of expectancy. You may wish to settle down with a large cup of hot chocolate on some snowy evening and read more about his complex studies, but for now let's simply look at his findings.

Vroom states that people bring certain expectations with them when they enter into any relationship. If those expectations are met, the person is satisfied and motivated. If the reality does *not* live up to the expectation, the person feels cheated, let down, and is de-motivated.

The purpose of mentioning Vroom here should be obvious. In marketing, you are working to establish a relationship. It is critical for that relationship, with its exchange of value for value, to be open, honest, and well defined so that the expectations are real on both sides. A major responsibility of the Volunteer Director is to see that expectations are met—those the volunteer has of the agency, and those the agency has of the volunteer. Another word for this is accountability—from both sides!

In recruitment, the best tool you have to make sure the expectation is accurate is the job design. The two other tools to keep reality in focus are the interview and the training prior to work.

In fundraising, the best tool you can have is proper survey and demographics results so that goals are set realistically with proper time frames and appropriate leadership.

In advocacy, the homework or research preparation is vital so that the right people and power sources are tapped at the right time for the right things.

Nothing can be more deadly than a marketing campaign that sets up false expectations in the minds of the potential consumers or the agency. When those expectations are not met, the consumer or agency feels "conned," misled, and angry. This, then negatively affects any long range planning, the building of lasting relationships, and trust between parties.

Vroom's theory and its implications, play a vital role in marketing success. Lack of understanding of this theory is very often what I find at the bottom of horror-stories in marketing. My admonition earlier in this book to *NEVER PROMISE WHAT YOU CAN'T DELIVER* has a direct correlation to Vroom's expectancy theory!

WHY PEOPLE GIVE

"Not he who has much is rich, but he who gives much."
. . . Eric Fromm

There are groups that annually track how people give their time and dollars on a voluntary basis. It is important to keep up with these statistics, and I urge you to do so annually. Remember, however, that when classifying all the reasons for giving, they come down to two general headings:

1. People give because they feel they will get something in return that they value (satisfaction, goods, reward, etc.) or

2. People give because of commitment to the asker.

In establishing trade relationships in marketing, you will have a higher ratio of success when you offer the person or group something they value, *and* you have a person to whom they have a commitment do the asking.

A list of reasons and patterns of giving will help you in establishing value exchanges:

1983 Contributions[5]

Individuals	$51.85 Billion	82.9%
Bequests	4.52 Billion	7.0%
Foundations	3.46 Billion	5.3%
Corporations	3.10 Billion	4.8%

1983 Distributions[5]

Religion	$31.03 Billion	47.8%
Health	9.15 Billion	14.1%
Education	9.04 Billiion	12.9%
Social Welfare	4.08 Billion	10.7%
Arts & Humanities	4.08 Billiion	6.3%
Civic Affairs	1.80 Billion	2.8%
Other	2.89 Billion	4.4%

REASONS PEOPLE VOLUNTEER[6]*

Want to help	45%
Interest in activity	35%
Enjoy work & feel needed	29%
Loved one in program	23%
Can express religious beliefs	21%

Can gain job/work experience	11% adults/20% teens
Can use free time	6%

*(People could check more than one answer, thus the reason for a total higher than 100%)

CONCLUSION

Step #3 (Who Has What You Need?) forces you to focus on what the agency needs, what people have as motivation, etc., and to begin to match the needs of both to choose which can be drawn together in an exchange relationship.

The answer to who has what you need and needs what you have to offer is not a simple one. The effective volunteer director must understand something about human and group motivation, must have enough specific information to target appropriate markets, must understand values, and then move beyond this theory to actually making a trade relationship happen.

CHAPTER FOUR — REFERENCES

1. Paul Hersey, and Kenneth Blanchard, *Management of Organizational Behavior,* Prentice Hall, 1972 (2nd ed.).
2. George Litwin and Robert Stringer, *Motivational and Organizational Climate,* Harvard University, 1968.
3. Ibid.
4. David hampton, Charles Summer and Ross Webber *Organizational Behavior and the Practice of Management,* Foresman and Co. 1973.
5. American Assn. of Fund Raising Council, *Giving,* N.Y. 1983.
6. Gallup Organization, *Volunteerism, Independent Sector,* Washington, D.C., 1983.
7. Paul Wagner, *Marketing for NPO's from a Practitioner's Point of View,* Marketing in Non-profit Organizations, Patrick Montana, Ed. AMACOM, 1978, p. 38.

The Fourth and Final Step: How Do You Get What You Need?

"You have not because you ask not."

*"Not all products can be placed on a shelf. Intangible products
need imaginative forms of differentiation because
they can seldom be experienced or tested in advance."*
. . . Theodore Levitt[1]

Step #4 in the process of successful marketing finally puts all the work of the previous three steps together—combining what you have as resources, what you know you need, and which markets can provide your need.

In order to understand how you acquire the resources to meet your needs, you must acquaint yourself with strategizing, a knowledge of what people really "buy," how to "ask," how to package your requests, and the importance of removing peoples objections.

STRATEGIZING

To strategize simply means to plan actions to accomplish your goals. Webster's New World Dictionary, Student's Edition (Prentice-Hall publisher) goes one step further by defining a strategy as *"clever* means of bringing something about."

MARKETING STRATEGIES

In the 1950's both Ford and Chevrolet introduced compact cars in an effort to compete with the smaller imports such as Volkswagen, Fiat, and Japanese autos that were beginning to grab a larger and larger share of the market.

Despite strong advertising efforts, the cars did not sell well. Ford, in response to this disappointment did a marketing survey regarding their car, the Falcon, and discovered which features were most appealing to buyers and who those buyers were.

Results of this survey showed sporty features, such as bucket seats, higher-powered engines, four-speeds, etc. were growing in popularity with younger buyers.

In 1965 Ford introduced both a new product and a new marketing approach, and in so doing, set the auto industry on its ear.

That product was the MUSTANG.

The marketing strategy was designed in line with what the market survey reported were the most wanted features: it was priced reasonably, it was promoted as a sports touring car for the young buyer, and it was available (distributed) everywhere.

The strategy took into account all four of the variables in marketing:

DEVELOP THE RIGHT *PRODUCT.*
SUPPORT IT WITH THE RIGHT *PROMOTION.*
PUT IT IN THE RIGHT *PLACE.*
AND AT THE RIGHT *PRICE.*

Please note that the key word in that golden rule is *RIGHT* . . . and reflects the strategy used to accomplish Ford's marketing goal. This same kind of success can be yours as you strategize efforts to win volunteers, supporters and donors.

STRATEGY OPTIONS

There are three possible strategies that an organization can adopt toward a market in which it has an interest. These strategies are known as UNDIFFERENTIATED marketing, CONCENTRATED marketing, and DIFFERENTIATED marketing.[2]

UNDIFFERENTIATED MARKETING: This occurs when an organization decides to treat the whole market as homogeneous. It does not concentrate on what is different about it, but rather what is alike. There is no attempt to segment the market as all.

Many agencies treat all potential volunteers the same—using one recruitment appeal ("fill your time," "work with kids" etc.) which assumes all people volunteer for the same reasons.

Organizations that have one point of view and work to sell it to everyone are actually engaging in undifferentiated marketing.

Groups who use one fundraising tool, such as an event, are actually trying to say that their one event has great and equal appeal to everyone. . . . .again "undifferentiated" marketing.

In sharing this strategy with you, I simply want you to recognize it. . . . I am not promoting it! It is usually ineffective and ignores the potential strength of modern marketing which pays close attention to market differences and individual needs.

An agency with "one cause" or "one message" has a very difficult path cut out for it, especially if it assumes that their way is the *only* way for everyone. This often leads to a bad guy/good guy attitude that defies all rules of "friend-raising."

For those groups whose sole purpose is to promote a singular idea, I urge careful consideration of promotion—so that you can differentiate between markets and tailor your presentations in non-accusatory, personalized wording that different markets might hear.

CONCENTRATED MARKETING: This strategy occurs when an organization does indeed divide markets into specific, identifiable segments, and then decides to put all its efforts into just one of those segments.

Usually this decision comes about when an agency decides it lacks the depth to spread itself over many segments, and so decides to concentrate its service to just one.

In volunteer programs this concentration may come about by recruiting only from the churches or service club sectors; for an agency, this may mean serving only seniors; for fundraising, it may mean only focusing on large donors (this is also called the "heavy-donor strategy" for fundraising).

Concentrated marketing, when done with thoroughness and consideration for price, package, and promotion, is usually quite successful.

The organization gets to know the concentrated market extremely well, even to the point of becoming an expert on it and accepted as part of the market itself. It also can become quite donor-efficient as it specializes in services in the most economical way (time, effort, money).

It will be important for your agency, should you choose concentrated marketing, to carefully select your target market. It should be relatively underserved, and you should be able to provide it with the services it needs.

DIFFERENTIATED MARKETING: When an organization decides to identify and serve two or more market segments at once, designing different products and/or marketing programs for each, this is considered differentiated marketing.

The purpose of this strategy is to have the greatest possible impact on each segment. It realizes that the same message to different markets will water down the effectiveness.

While National Director for Project Concern International (a charity serving health care needs of the children of poverty through hospitals, nutrition centers, schools etc.) I learned the importance of "packaging" our approach for help to different markets:

For the medical profession, I spoke of the fact that we delivered primary health care when needed, but concentrated on preventative care through instruction for mothers on nutrition, through a five year training program for paramedicals who could take over in remote areas when we left etc. I provided statistics on decreases in infant mortality rates after our training and health care delivery by our trained paramedics, to back up my appeal.

For the educators from whom we needed permission for school assemblies to promote our cause, we spoke about the number of mothers trained in our nutrition centers, the education provided clients to help them break the poverty cycle, the top notch training of paramedics, and the value of their school children learning about international poverty. Statistics and studies backed up all our claims.

Obviously, Project Concern was using a differentiated marketing strategy as it "packaged" its donor and volunteer appeals differently for different markets.

96

The motivation for an organization using this strategy is varied:

1. It hopes for greater effectiveness in serving its clients.

2. It hopes for greater response from donors and volunteers.

3. It hopes for greater loyalty due to the fact that what it offers is tailored to each segment's needs and wants.

The challenge of differentiated marketing is that you often find different segments in conflict with one another (public and private health care facilities, etc.) and your marketing will need to be carefully orchestrated (as discussed in Chapter III.)

CHOOSING A STRATEGY

The choice of a marketing strategy depends on the circumstances that impact the agency or program:

1. *Resources*—if limited, concentrated marketing is probably the choice, so that your dollars can be most effectively used.

2. *Homogeneous Market*—if your market is pretty much the same in needs, wants, etc. it would be foolish to try to segment it. (Example: When our village asks for volunteers and donations for the annual 4th of July fireworks display, recruiters go door to door, knowing that most townspeople will want to support the effort.)

3. *Desire for Leadership*—if your group decides it wants to be a leader in several segments of the market, it will choose differentiated marketing.

4. *Competition*—if competitors have already established a dominance in several segments of the market, you may wish to concentrate on those untargeted segments.

MARKETING VARIABLES

As mentioned previously, in relating the marketing success of the Mustang there are four strategic marketing variables:[3]

PRODUCT
PRICE
PLACE
PROMOTION

Each of these variables carries several options in marketing circles that can be translated to your work as Volunteer Directors. Let's look at each.

PRODUCT

There are three things you can do about a product:

1. Introduce a new product.
2. Change or modify an existing product.
3. Withdraw a product.

Introduction of a new product: It is important to try to introduce new "products" regularly—offering new volunteer jobs, new ways to support, new opportunities for involvement. As the world changes around you, seek creative ways to involve people and groups:

1. Families volunteering as a unit.
2. Job sharing between working volunteers.
3. Flex-space for people confined in nursing homes, rehabilitation sites, penal institutions so that volunteer work can be taken to them in their place of residence.
4. Volunteer opportunities for 2nd and 3rd shift workers.
5. Jobs for single parents that provide parallel child care, etc.

All of these are "new products."

Remember that you are in a highly competitive business—the volunteer's time, like the donor's dollars, will be spent where the best value is received. New products that make it possible for people to be involved will strengthen your marketing strategy immensely.

Modifying old: The purpose in modifying an old product is to extend its life.

One approach to modifying a product or effort is to find a new use for it. In volunteer terms you may no longer need volunteers to come to your church office to type and run stencils for the weekly newsletter because the church has computerized the effort and hired a computer technician.

These same people (with typing and clerical skills, etc.) can be utilized in other areas of church work, such as recording information from volunteer survey results, telephoning shut-ins, etc.

Another approach to modification is examination of when and where you offer your opportunities and changing factors to suit the market. Many women's organizations are alive today because they changed the hour they met, the place of assembly, and the focus of the group from entertainment to personal development.

LIFE CYCLES

Every product has a *life cycle* and so do volunteer and donor opportunities as they reach market saturation.

In an earlier chapter, I shared that a charity I worked with became dependent on one fundraising event. After the introduction of this event (new to the United States) in the late 60's, the growth rate of participation and financial return was incredible. In the mid seventies maximum profit levels were reached signaling maturity. As saturation and decline set in, the profit (both in participation and donor dollars) declined.

In an effort to cut the losses the event was modified, but it still declined . . . not because the efforts of modification were weak, but because it had reached its saturation point, and thus the end of its life cycle.

The efforts to point out the life cycle theory were rejected as "alarmist," and the charity continued to work hard to sell the event. This continued to involve people for a time, although less donations were realized per participant and finally participation declined.

The Product Life Cycle was diagramed by Cohen and Reddish[4] and can offer Nonprofits great insight into programs, cause, or event saturation. I have taken the liberty of substituting words more familiar to the field of Volunteer Management that their original terms of dollars, sales, and profit and adapted the following diagram to explain the Life Cycle:

I introduce this "life cycle" understanding here, as too frequently I see people beating on a dead horse by trying to promote the same event, program, or volunteer job *long* after the market has been saturated or the need has disappeared.

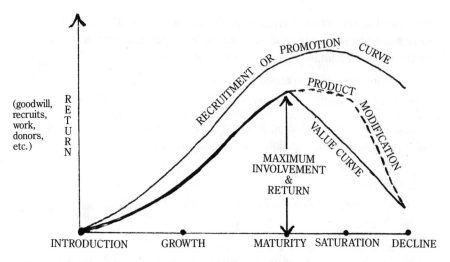

Figure 1.

If, after modifying a specific product, you still see decline in the value returned to your program, do not label it a failure—simply understand the product life cycle of any effort and move on to something new!

Withdrawing a Product: In their book, *Successful Marketing for Small Businesses,*[5] Cohen and Reddich state, "While every businessperson must use judgment in running their business, they should not allow their emotions or their personal prejudices to cloud their judgmental faculties."

If you can translate those words into the field of volunteer mangement, you can see their wisdom and application.

There are simply times when an effort needs to be withdrawn! Too frequently, when I question the validity of a method, job, event, etc. the program directors and leaders begin their rebuttal with "But we always . . ."

There are many efforts that are going on, taxing energies and resources, that are simply inappropriate for the realities of today and need to be dropped. (That can be a real challenge if the effort's founder is still on your board and can't see why you need to drop their bandage-rolling committee that was all the rage in 1918!)

Continually review the efforts you are making to see if they indeed are fitting in with the agency goals *and* available resources. Do not

100

consider the dropping of an effort a "negative" at all; it's simply a way to release physical, financial, and creative resource energies to other, more needed, efforts.

PRICING

The pricing consideration as a strategic variable is critical for volunteer programs and translates into what it will cost participants in terms of:

1. energy
2. out of pocket costs (gas, food, etc.)
3. time
4. emotions

There are many excellent "products" offered by nonprofits that are rejected because one or more aspects of the price is too high. Examples might be:

— Volunteer jobs to rock children in a hospital (a job most people love). The hospital, however, is in a very bad section of town, no public transportation is available, parking lots are unlit and far removed from the buildings. The price (safety) is too high!

— A professional association offers a highly demanded credentialling. The instructions on how to proceed are very complex and confusing: the workshops required to begin the process are few and far between and the required written work takes two years. The price is considered by most, too high!

— A charity makes a mass appeal to potential donors to support a child in a foreign land for one year. Only a full year's sponsorship is acceptable ($240.00) and the "adopters" must also comply with a list of support efforts for each of the twelve months *and* report their results to the parent organization. In many ways, the price is too high!

These are real-life examples of inappropriate pricing for outstanding products or efforts.

PLACING

Placing as a strategic variable can mean the decisions you make regarding the best distribution channels to use in getting your messages known to the people who might respond to them. (It can also refer to the place in which they can *do* their volunteering.)

Understand that you will be competing with other agencies, charities, groups, etc. for effective use of distribution channels and that some will be more effective than others for your messages.

UNDER NO CIRCUMSTANCES EVER ALLOW YOUR PROGRAM TO SURVIVE THROUGH USE OF ONLY *ONE* DISTRIBUTION CHANNEL! Spread your message through as many as possible. Check your Resource File (Chapter II) for people already involved with you who themselves have access to distribution channels (clubs, media, newsletters, company bulletin boards, granting agencies, etc.).

AN EXERCISE IN IDENTIFYING DISTRIBUTION CHANNELS:

1. Gather top people from your agency to brainstorm.

2. List potential sites where people (who might wish to be involved with you as donors, volunteers, supporters, etc.) might be found.

3. Under each grouping (market) list ways to reach them.

4. Compare these lists with available resource connections in your Resource File.

5. Ask brainstormers to think of ways to tap into these channels.

6. Map out plans for use of these channels.

PROMOTION

There are three components in promotional variables:

1. Special promotion campaigns

2. Personal selling

3. Advertising

Special promotions are specific campaigns, which can be done throughout the agencies' life cycle, and are targeted for a specific goal (recruitment, fundraising campaign, community awareness, etc.). The promotion's goal is to gain a greater market share in terms of volunteers, public awareness, programs, goods or dollars.

Personal selling is a strategy I talk about at length in discussing the art of asking. I admit to a prejudice that this personalized selling strategy—individual recruitment, donor appeals, etc.,—is the most effective in the long run.

The volunteer or donor, who knowingly accepts the role of "agent" for your group and excites others to the point of wanting to become involved, is an example of effective personal selling. There is no more effective recruiter than a satisfied volunteer (and none worse than a dissatisfied one!)

Advertising will be discussed in the following chapter extensively and therefore skipped here for all practical purposes. To set the stage, however, let me share that in determining advertising (or PR) efforts, you will need to consider what medium to use, (print, visual, etc.), which media outlets to tap, and when to advertise.

PEOPLE DON'T BUY "PRODUCTS!" They Buy Solutions to Problems

In his book, *The Marketing Imagination,* Theodore Levitt[6] states "A product has no value until it has a customer. Customers want products that will solve their problems."

Good marketers understand that people really don't buy products; they buy solutions and satisfactions.

Levitt points out that you don't sell 1/4" drill bits; you give people a way to make 1/4" holes. He also shares that "Henry Ford's unique insight was that the potential buyer's problem was getting enough money to buy a car. Ford used the marketing imagination to solve the problem by finding a way to make cars more cheaply."[2]

All of this marketing insight can be translated into the work of the volunteer director through the understanding that people volunteer for many different reasons. These reasons are needs, as discussed in Chapter IV, and are as strong as people's needs for 1/4" holes or inexpensive cars.

As I travel around the U.S. and Canada, asking audiences what reasons they are seeing for people volunteering, a typical list emerges:

1. Repay a debt—loved one helped, volunteer after being a client, feel sense of duty to country, etc.

2. Tradition—family, club, group, church, etc.

3. Counterpoint—it's totally *different* from their paid work— serves as a relief and change of pace.

4. Keep skills sharp—retirees wanting to keep working skills sharp, skilled artist who can't work in their trade temporarily, professional women home raising a family, etc.

5. Religious reasons—want to put their faith into action.

6. Relationships—single parent wants to have work with child, parents want to work as family to set role-model, singles want to meet new people etc.

7. Values—people want chance to meet and work with others with like values, etc.

8. Fun—people want to enjoy themselves.

9. Tax benefit—people want tax benefit the effort can offer.

10. Exposure—people want opportunity to meet specific people (boss, potential employer, client, club leader, celebrity, etc.) on a one to one basis, with the hope of establishing a relationship.

11. Skill, experience, resume building—to gain skills and document them.

12. Fill time—many people are weighted down by too much time on their hands. Volunteering fills that time with worthwhile activity.

13. Self worth—association with a "good" program can help people feel better about themselves. People who consider themselves "losers" can desperately need to feel they are part of a "winning" agency.

It may be stretching it to say these reasons for volunteering are problems seeking solutions, but certainly they are needs looking for satisfactions, yearnings needing fulfillment, and perceived "gaps" looking to be filled.

In the movie *Rocky*, the lead character is asked why he feels he and his girlfriend fell in love, given their vast differences. The reply simply was, "She's got gaps and I've got gaps, and we fill each others gaps."

In essence, this is marketing—to fill each others gaps and to understand that the successful exchange relationship in marketing comes about when you offer someone a solution to their problem or need—an opportunity to fill their "gap."

THE ART OF ASKING

There is a secret to the art of asking, one that seems to have been kept from most people who are assigned the task of asking others to donate their energies, time, dollars, or goods.

This secret is the true "magic" of marketing and is the reversal of people's normal approach to making requests:

YOU ARE NOT TRYING TO TALK PEOPLE INTO SAYING "YES" . . . YOU ARE TRYING TO *REMOVE* PEOPLE'S REASONS TO SAY "NO."

Too frequently people try to arm-twist and convince others to say "yes," rather than diagnosing possible objections and removing them so that nothing prevents a positive response to recruitment or donor requests.

THE HIDDEN QUESTIONS

There are certain "hidden questions" that most people have as they are approached by volunteer recruiters. It is critical that these common questions—which if unanswered become a "no"—are known to anyone assigned the task of "asking" so that they can build the answers into their presentations:

1. What do you want from me? (To do, give, support, etc.)

2. How much will I be required to give? (Time, energy, money, goods, etc.)

3. What do I get in return? (Satisfactioin, needs, wants, etc.)

4. Why should I trust you? (Reputation, cause, credibility, etc.)

There may be more specific questions that need to be answered and objections that need to be removed as you ask directly, but these four general questions should be considered as standard and their answers well-prepared.

ASKING TECHNIQUES

There are four ways in which you can "ask" for anything. In order of *de*scending effectiveness, they are:

1. *In Person Method—One to One:* This is the most effective technique as it is eyeball to eyeball and therefore the most forceful. The request can be personalized and flexible, depending on feedback. It is most effective when the asker is known to the person being asked, and is trusted by them. Strengths of this method are that it:

   a. Lends urgency to the appeal.

   b. Establishes a relationship between parties.

   c. Gets easier with practice.

   d. Produces more and larger results.

   e. Offers direct communications to remove reasons to say "NO."

   f. Can diagnose objections.

   g. Can redirect support if the person is reluctant in one area but wanting to help in others.

2. *Group Asking Method—*This is the second most effective technique which has one person speaking to a group of people as they seek support. The "asker" explains the need, shares their own commitment, tells the group what they can do to help and what is being asked of them. The presentation uses phrases familiar to the group (their language, slogans, etc.) and shares the benefits that will be returned to them. The appeal is *always* asked in terms of the clients served, *NOT* the agency (you ask for help for Red Cross disaster victims, *NOT* the Red Cross).

Try to use audio-visuals in the presentation to show clients being served and help the audience get a "feel" for the work being done.

If you choose this method of one-to-group, take along several others from your program (preferably volunteers) so that as you spot people in the audience interested in your requests, they can help you follow up with individual conversations.

When you see people in a group highly attentive (watch body language and eye contact) to your presentation, be sure to talk to them individually before you leave, getting their name, phone number, and interest recorded for follow-up within a few days. Try to make a specific appointment with them on the spot and then BE SURE TO FOLLOW-UP WITH THE PROMISED CONTACT! At the very least pass around a sign up sheet to allow people to indicate interest.

This technique still affords the vital feedback link and individual contacts so important in the art of asking and effective marketing.

BE SURE TO DO YOUR HOMEWORK before speaking to a group. Check your resource file or call their president or program chair, to know who the leadership is, when their fiscal year ends, what their past giving patterns are, any interaction history between your agency and them, what competition you have for their support, their purpose, creed, and structure, etc., and any available general information on member characteristics (ages, occupation, etc.).

One of the most deadly things that can happen to you as you make a presentation is to come uninformed, making errors that detract from your mission and probably sink your chances for support before it's even requested!

3. *Request by Telephone*—This method is more impersonal as it brings no eye contact, therefore eliminating the pressure that eye contact brings on a potential donor.

   There are four type of phone requests and usually are rated for potential success as follows:

   Most Successful: Called *knows caller* and *cause*.

   Some Success: Called *knows caller* but not cause.

   Less Success: Caller *knows cause* but not caller.

   Least Successful: Caller *does not* know caller or cause.

Obviously, if you must rely on a phone campaign, target your calls to markets that know your work or cause, *and* recruit callers who know the people personally.

4. *Direct Mail Approach*—This is the least effective of the four techniques, and puts the request in writing. The "success rating" used for phone calls in the previous phoning method can be used in ranking potential effectiveness of mail request.

Please understand what direct mail campaigns really are—shotgun approaches to as wide a public (i.e.: the telephone directory!) as possible in order to gain the normal response level of 1-3% of the mailing. This 1-3% is then turned into a list of interested people who are then contacted regularly.

Keep in mind the definition of marketing, which is *targeted*. Direct mail is a shotgun approach which is trying to sift out future marketing targets.

A targeted letter appeal is more in line with marketing strategies, and in some cases is highly appropriate. A general appeal, however, is impersonal, easy to say "NO" to, usually unsolicited, does not take the reader's needs into account, and does not offer feedback.

HOW PEOPLE RELATE

I'm going to take a chance on your ability to stick with me on a subject that may, to many volunteer directors seem a bit too "deep" and "high-pressured". I introduce it here because I can recall a few instances when I had to get the support of a specific person and had to really *work* to gain their cooperation. Had I known the following, my job would have been much easier!

There are three primary ways in which people relate to one another.[7] In asking, this is vital information to have so that the most positive of the three can be used. Although more frequently seen in fundraising examples, they can also be seen in recruitment interactions:

1. *Dominance:* move *against* each other with aggression and hostility.
2. *Detachment:* move *away* from each other, remaining aloof and indifferent.
3. *Dependency:* move *toward* each other with warmth and friendliness.

In meeting people in each category, you will need to understand what their reaction will be to the recruiter, what personal hidden question each will have, and what the best approach might be to win them over. The following chart outlines all three considerations:

Let's look more closely at the best approaches for each of the three categories of prospects. Again, although these may seem to be more relevant to fundraising efforts, volunteer directors may find them useful as they try to recruit key people or seek support for an effort:

	DOMINANT	DETACHED	DEPENDENT
Reaction to asker	Fight	Avoid	Welcome
Hidden question	Are you good enough?	Are you logical?	Do you care?
Best approach	Smooth dominance	Facts and logic	Friendly dominance

1. *Smooth Dominance for Dominant Prospects:*

These people often surround themselves with status symbols and trappings, may keep you waiting for an appointment, and can often have secretaries that let you know the boss is more important than you!

Often, upon entering their office, they will not look up—being just "too busy." They shake hands firmly and look you straight in the eye. They often tell you where to sit and try to control the situation with direct questions and statements.

Your Approach:

Make your opening brisk and business-like, keeping non-threatening eye contact at all times. Make sure your voice is strong and confident; speak in short sentences. Do not smile too much (they often think that's a sign of weakness). Avoid details. Use assertive gestures. Show respect for their position and time. Don't grovel. Show them you are good enough to deserve their energies in your program and make your presentation. Never go over the time allotted, and follow up immediately on requests.

2. *Facts and Logic for Detached Prospects:*

Their Characteristics:

These people create an impersonal environment for themselves, and their homes and offices usually reflect this by being rather sterile. Secretaries tend to be cold and impersonal; when you come into their office they usually do not establish eye contact until the last moment—and then it is very brief. A handshake is usually at the greatest distance possible and very brief and cool. You will probably not be invited to sit down, and in fact, they seem disinterested in what you're doing. They listen but contribute little, giving almost no feedback.

Your Approach.

Make your opening very brief and rather impersonal. Do not demand eye contact. Do not talk too much or too fast, and leave long pauses to afford them a chance to comment. Avoid personal remarks and don't gesture too much. Don't try to be "folksy" or "cute." Concentrate on giving facts and make your presentation in a clear, logical, and outlined form. Watch the time so that you do not take more than your allotment. Offer written materials, facts, figures, and references during the meeting and afterward, if requested.

3. *Friendly Dominance for Dependent Prospects:*

Their Characteristics:

Such people usually create a very warm, personalized, friendly atmosphere in their home and office. Furnishings are comfortable, and rooms are decorated with photos, personal items, their children/grandchildren's drawings, etc. Their secretaries usually call the boss by a first name and offer you a warm, friendly greeting when you approach.

The prospect will often come out to the waiting room to greet you and escort you in. Eye contact comes immediately and continues in a very warm and friendly (non-threatening) way. They project concern and caring for you and usually want you to be seated where you are most comfortable. Frequently, if space permits, they have informal "conversation areas" in their offices, and you can sense that they hope you'll want to sit with them there.

Their handshake is long, warm, and they often grip your arm or shoulder with the other hand, in a friendly but appropriate manner.

Your Approach:

Your opening should be warm, friendly, and unhurried, conveying warmth and concern through smiles and eye contact. Lean forward when talking and offer strong gestures while speaking. Let them talk and listen attentively, mentioning something they said in your next statement. Quote them, if possible, to win points. Talk about your personal commitment to the cause and tell stories of people served. Proceed into your request, using anecdotes and references to the clients who need them. Be honest, sincere, and project your natural warmth and caring. Remember the golden rule—NEVER TRY TO CON A "CARER!" They'll spot you in a second and smile as they close the door behind you.

The approach to the last of the three types—Dependent Prospects—will probably seem the most natural for you and will be typical of most people you encounter. You will, however, need to be ready for the other two types, and tailor your asking to suit their acceptance level.

This is simply another application of differentiation and also draws on your understanding of motivation—especially McClelland's Motivational Classifications which can parallel many attitudes of POWER (Dominant), ACHIEVEMENT (Detached), and AFFILIATION (Dependent).

ASKING FOR VOLUNTEERS

The process of "asking" when you are trying to get people to volunteer their time and energies is of course more commonly called "recruitment".

The actual asking is part of the interview process conducted most effectively, on a one to one basis and is outlined in Marlene Wilson's book, "The Effective Management of Volunteer Programs".

This interview process . . . mentioned previously in Chapter III—is defined by Mrs. Wilson as "a conversation with a purpose" . . . in this case, the purpose is to enlist people as volunteers.

During this asking process, you, as the asker, work to:

1. Establish a rapport with the potential recruit, relaxing them and hopefully identifying a common link between you.

2. Explain the work of the agency in terms of helping people.

3. Answer any questions the prospect has.

4. Using non-directive questioning, find out about the needs, motivations, gifts, experiences, likes, demands, etc. of the prospect.

5. Sketch opportunities for service that the agency has, noting any responses by the prospect. The jobs you list need to correspond (if possible) to the needs, skills etc. just related to you by the prospect.

6. Give the prospect plenty of time to talk . . . avoid monopolizing the conversation and avoid all assumptions.

7. If you are interviewing for placement (rather than a screening interview) share job designs of specific assignments, being willing to modify aspects of the design if needed while still making the work effective for the agency.

8. Ask for a specific commitment (outlined in job design) and make sure the recruit understands where the job fits in the overall work of the agency.

9. Speak in terms of clients served . . . even if their job does not directly deal with clients. Example: You are recruiting someone to set up a filing system in the agency office. Help the person understand that that system will enable the agency staff to serve clients more effectively through easily retrievable data and records. If possible, relate an actual incident that demonstrates your point.

10. Do *not* try to talk the recruits into a job if they seem legitimately reluctant about it. If no job opportunity interests them, set up a time of further contact . . . or . . . refer them to another agency you feel might utilize their gifts immediately.

11. Remember the "hidden questions" listed before and answer them in your conversation. Diagnose any "nos" they might have additionally and work to remove those you can. NEVER PROMISE TO REMOVE AN OBJECTION THAT YOU REALLY CANNOT . . . one major purpose beyond placement is the establishment of TRUST . . . something that cannot happen when you start off with a false promise!

12. If you cannot come to an agreement, thank them for their time, offer to keep in touch if that is their desire, and remember you are "friendraising" when you help the prospect feel valuable even though they will not be a part of your efforts.

13. Follow up on any promise . . . for more information, contacts, etc.

14. If the prospect does agree to become a recruit, establish this agreement in writing, either through the sharing of a formalized job design or more informally, through a personal note of thanks for their commitment. Set a time for a next meeting, the start of work or further contact, so the recruit is not left dangling.

This interview process . . . the actual "asking" . . . is critical, as it can set the tone of further trust, communication, understanding and enabling. The key is a caring, knowledgeable interviewer, skilled in the arts of non-directive questioning, motivation and listening!

ASKING FOR FUNDRAISING

In fundraising, there are four steps in the actual asking process when you are eyeball to eyeball. Each one is important and their sequence is vital.

1. *The Opening:* This is where you create interest, build a rapport, offer credibility, link them to your cause, and speak their language.

2. *The Case:* Tell your story, avoid arm twisting, express what is needed by clients, offer benefits, outline what is needed (time, money, energy, etc.), what value they might receive from involvement, diagnose any "nos," and remove them honestly. NEVER REMOVE AN OBJECTION DISHONESTLY—that's a form of promising something you can't deliver . . . a marketing "NO-NO!"

3. *Close:* You wouldn't believe how many people get through steps #1 and #2 and then just sit back, hoping the prospect will somehow volunteer assistance they think you need. Be assertive— *ask* specifically and close the agreement. Summarize benefits, establish urgency, list support they will receive if recruited as a volunteer, build in a follow-up meeting and keep control of the conversation.

4. *Follow-up:* Always follow-up a meeting with a thank you. One top fundraiser was asked upon his retirement, to what he attributed his great success. "Simple," he replied. "I always hand wrote my thank yous, and I always sent them to everyone." Even if the person turns your request down. Thank them for their time and attention. Remember you are in the business of

"friend-raising!" If the person asks for more information or materials send them immediately.

DANGERS IN ASKING

There are certain dangers in the asking process that you need to be aware of. They are:

1. Assuming anything! (DON'T)
2. Jumping to conclusions.
3. Categorizing people too quickly.
4. Controlling too much.
5. Talking too much.
6. Hearing only what you wish to hear.
7. Not honestly listening or feeding back.
8. Interrupting.
9. Questions/statements too long and complex.
10. Incongruence between words and body language.

THINGS TO AVOID IN ASKING

There are several "no-nos" in asking; ones that will usually cause the prospect to mistrust or back off from you. They are:

1. *Bail out Plea*—Who wants a free ticket on the Titanic anyway?
2. *Conning*—My grandmother always told me I'd get black spots on my tongue if I lied, and I wouldn't even risk grey ones by conning. IT CATCHES UP WITH YOU!
3. *Guilt*—Telling prospects a child will die if you don't become involved is a little heavy and makes more enemies than friends.
4. *Aggressiveness*—Assertive, yes; aggressive, no. If you don't know the difference, find out! Most people want to sense your confidence, not your ability to tear their heads off should they refuse you.
5. *Negativism*—Don't think you can build yourself up by tearing others down. You can't, and besides, the CEO of that "other" you're tearing down could be your prospect's dear Aunt Maude!

6. *Blaming*—Weak people blame, strong people solve problems, seeing them as challenges. You want to be strong, so avoid the "blame game."

DIAGNOSING OBJECTIONS

If you accept the premise that you are not trying to talk people into saying "yes," but are actually trying to remove people's reasons to say "no" to your marketing efforts, you need to be equipped with information on how to diagnose potential "nos."

Earlier we looked at the hidden questions people have as they consider volunteer opportunities. These questions relate to specifics of work—what, when, how long, value return, etc.

In addition to these questions, all of which can be categorized under the heading of "clarity," there are seven types of objections[8] you might hear as you approach prospects for volunteer jobs, support, or donations. Let's look at each and what to do about them.

THE STALL

In this type of objection, the prospect tries to postpone action. Some stalls are legitimate ("I'm not ready to take on that job until school starts in the fall"), but many are really rationalizations to help people avoid commitment. Often this is a fear of failure and needs to be countered with specifics on how to do the job, what success is, and the importance of immediate response to help the most clients.

THE BIG "D"—DOUBT

Doubts frequently indicate a lack of confidence in you, your agency, or the job to be done. Your prospect may question whether you can really deliver what you promise, or if your agency can really impact the cause it seeks to serve.

The answer to this objection is to offer proof of your claims—client statistics, audits, volunteer endorsements, etc.

REQUESTS FOR REASSURANCE—"Don't Let Me Goof!"

Many people want reassurarnce that becoming involved with you will not be a mistake and that you really care about them as individuals. These objections are usually masked because people don't like to admit they need reassurance. Offer them proof of past accomplishments, invite them to speak to key volunteers, and reassure them in order to remove this objection. It often helps to carefully outline the training and support they will receive in preparation for their work.

"COAX ME"

Some people may wish to be coaxed out of a need to feel more wanted or valuable. Others may want you to convince them because they have a hard time making a decision. If, indeed, you know this person can be of value to your program *and* you have a value trade to offer in return, you may wish to apply gentle, positive pressure. BE CAREFUL HOWEVER—Don't step over the limits of coaxing into "arm-twisting" . . . you may end up with a right person in a wrong job!

HIDDEN AGENDA

A really tough challenge comes as you encounter resistance for reasons that remain hidden. When you encounter this, probe gently to uncover it—then answer it directly. Understand that hidden objections can often be layered under stated (but not the real) objections (i.e.: "I'm too busy" masks the hidden objection of "I don't trust you"). Two clues that you are encountering hidden objections are 1) illogical statements (i.e.: a bored retiree says they have no time; a wealthy person says they can't afford something, etc.) 2) "no-by-domino"—when you answer one objection they give you another, repeating this pattern through a dozen "nos." All you can do is *try* to get to the real objection and attempt to remove it. Please know that frequently you *cannot* uncover the real objection—when this happens, simply accept what they are saying, thank them and move on.

MISTAKEN OBJECTIONS

These are objections based on inaccurate or incomplete information. Clarification of the misinformation is the answer to this problem. Try to do this verbally and visually (charts, graphs, goal statements, etc.) so that they are impacted more strongly with the truth than with the bad information.

HARD OBJECTIONS

A request on the part of the prospect that you provide benefits you really do not offer is called a "hard" objection. In other words, they want *more* than you have to give. When this happens, resist the temptation to offer anything to win their support. ONLY OFFER WHAT YOU CAN HONESTLY *DELIVER!*

One agency really lost ground in credibility, support, etc. when the founder promised to start a new type of program (drug rehabilitation) in order to gain funds and volunteers for his poverty-relief charity.

The charity could not afford to set up a new program, did not have expertise in the field, and was not chartered for that purpose. The founder had to retract his promise, the group withdrew its support, and the charity's reputation suffered dramatically as their credibility diminished.

CLARIFYING OBJECTIONS

In addition to classifying objections, it is critical for you to *clarify* them as to what they are and what they are *not.*

Assuming, without real probing, what a potential "no" is and building your proposal around that assumption is a very dangerous sport. If you've diagnosed incorrectly, you will be wasting your time and energies and that of your prospect.

KNOW WHAT THE PROBLEM IS—KNOW WHAT IT'S *NOT!*

ANSWERING OBJECTIONS

In every instance of having to answer objections be sure to answer confidently. Keep good, non-threatening eye contact, insure your expression and body language are congruent with your words, answer honestly, keep answers short and to the point, use caring words that personalize your response. In short, ENABLE people to believe your answers.

Also, keep in mind the subtle differences between interviewing volunteers for placement and asking donors for support. The former is much more gentle—the latter more pressurized!

MARKETING PROBLEMS
COMMON MARKETING ERRORS IN NON-PROFITS

There are several errors that seem to show up regularly in nonprofit groups as they try to incorporate marketing in their plans.

1. *WRONG STARTING POINT*

Many groups start from self interest rather than the needs of the client or volunteer. The focus seems to be on what is best for the agency. An example of this is the group that hears funds are available under a specific grant. They then write a proposal to fit the requirements of the funding agency irregardless of the needs of clients.

2. *DEALING WITH NON-NEEDS*

A second common error is the group that assumes it knows what is needed without bothering to confirm their assumptions. This type of agency, with its experts on leave from Mt. Olympus, never does a needs survey, is sure "we know what's best for THEM," and can't understand why they are losing volunteers, funds, support, and clients. Frequently their energies are aimed at 20 year old perceptions of needs that are inaccurate and often assessed from ivory tower perspectives.

3. *INACCURATE SELF-PERCEPTION—THE BETTER MOUSETRAP FOLLY*

The third and final common error is a belief by an agency that *only* they have the answers to problems, *only* they can provide people with something of worth, that they are *totally* unique. This causes this type group to feel everyone will automatically beat a path to their door, thus eliminating a need for marketing.

Such groups think that their "better mousetrap" will not have to be promoted, priced, or placed. WRONG!

BLOCKS TO MARKETING SUCCESS

There are six situations that can block successful efforts to implement marketing magic in your programs. They are:

1. *Lack of adequate funds for market research.* This prevents good information to guide decisions on product, price, promotion, and placement of efforts.

2. *Lack of understanding, and even resistance, in leaders for the need for marketing.* Marketing is frequently a major shift in thinking and introduces a need for much new learning. Old Abe

Maslow gives us a large clue to what is really behind resistance when he tells us, "Refusal to learn is more deeply a refusal to do."

3. *Total lack of marketing expertise or low status of staff who does have this expertise.* It is quite rare when board members understand marketing *or* understand how marketing skills they *do* have can be related to volunteer work.

4. *Lack of respect for promotion of any type.* Don't go into cardiac arrest if, when you first introduce marketing strategies, you are forbidden to use the words of marketing language! Many people in volunteer programs consider any form of promotion "hucksterism," "con-games," etc.

5. *Too many nonprofits think only on a short term basis.* Marketing is frequently a long term proposition, especially where reputation, attitudes, etc. are concerned. Marketing rarely offers a "quick fix" or instant answers to problems. The four steps of marketing take time and short cuts almost always minimize success.

6. *Professional marketers may not understand the complexities of the social issues faced by nonprofit service groups utilizing the volunteer resource.* Because of this, when such people are asked to consult with our groups, there tends to be an oversimplification of suggestions and a lack of respect for volunteer directors or nonprofit's veterans' knowledge.

When these problems arise and are identified, those in charge need to stop and intervene so that they are resolved and their blockage removed from future success.

MARKETING DEMAND LEVELS

During the life cycle of marketing efforts, you may find several different levels of demands that require different responses. Eight such levels are:

1. *Negative Demand* (People *reject* and resist you)—One response is to convert the rejection attitude into more positive response. You will need to address attitudes, enlist proponents to convince their peers of your worth, choose promotional avenues carefully, etc. A second response can be a thorough market research

that confirms what you are offering is really no longer wanted/ needed. At that point you drop it!

2. *No Demand* (People simply don't seek your offerings—a rather neutral, non-relationship)—The response is to stimulate demand—to convince people that what you have to offer is valuable. (Again, however, make sure what you offer really *is* still valuable!)

3. *Latent Demand* (People demand things you do not offer)—The response to this is to develop products or services to respond to this demand IF IN FACT THE SERVICE IS IN LINE WITH YOUR GOAL AND DELIVERY ABILITY. This is a real opportunity for the innovator to shine as they create new programs to meet this demand.

4. *Faltering Demand* (People demand less than before for products and services—a common event in volunteerism)—New plans for marketing need to be devised: new approaches, new places to offer opportunities, greater flexibility to attract new consumers. Thorough surveys of consumer needs and wants plus product structure and promotion is vital.

5. *Irregular Demand* (This demand fluctuates by season, timing, or other external factors that cause an irregular pattern of consumption.)—The task before an agency that is experiencing this type of demand is called "synchromarketing" which works to build a better balance to demand. Lesser demand volunteer jobs, for instance, might be enhanced through more tangible benefits; "off-season" (summer) might be targeted to more youth, who have summers free and could earn "credit" for school, etc.

6. *Full Demand* (This exists when the current level of demand is equal to delivery services.)—When this rare situation occurs, the danger is to think the marketing job is finished. Marketing is a dynamic effort, changing day by day and needs to be monitored constantly. The correct response to full demand is that you do everything to maintain this balance, keeping your finger on the pulse of demands, needs, responses, etc.

7. *Overfull Demand* (More demand than can be met)—When there are more demands than can be filled, the challenge is to demarket your efforts, cutting down on demands and bringing them into

reality. I am not suggesting you discourage people from volunteering, donating, or helping, but I do suggest you turn these people to different avenues of sharing. It is deadly to set up an expectation in a person's mind that they are needed and can be utilized and then *not* really do so. No amount of "busy work" will hide the fact that people are not *really* needed and a vicious cycle of damaged trust, negative-recruitment, and lack of credibility for the cause itself may have begun.

8. *Un-wholesome Demand* (A demand for something that is basically considered unhealthy.)—The response to this type of demand is "unselling" or discouraging people from wanting something. Many groups during the Viet Nam era tried to "unsell" that war; other agencies work to "unsell" drugs, cigarettes, and alcohol, etc. On a less obvious level, we can have demands in our volunteer programs for efforts that are no longer in the best interest of the agency or clients. We know, for instance, that volunteer visitors that helped keep heart attack victims content with confinement and non-activity were really hurting such clients and that return to activities as soon as possible is healthier. In such a case, marketing jobs that support this non-activity is detrimental.

CONCLUSION

The fourth step toward successful marketing has now been put in place—HOW DO YOU GET WHAT YOU NEED?

In this chapter you have looked at marketing variables, strategies, the arts of asking, removing "nos," and filling each other's gaps.

You have come a long way from step #1 where you identified your resources, passing through need identification and market targeting to tell you who has what you need.

Translation is constantly required as you apply marketing principles to the efforts of nonprofit service organizations and tap the strengths, energies, and resources of volunteers to carry out your work.

The magic of marketing is the caring concern for the values given to the volunteer and those received by the client.

When those concerns dominate actions, and people are asked to help clients, not organizations or events, the magic spreads itself like sunshine across the efforts and future of such groups.

Marketing for volunteer programs can be the magic tool to unlock the resources so badly needed by clients. It can also afford people the opportunity to give of themselves, and in return, receive incalculable benefits of satisfaction and pride in their accomplishments.

When marketing is defined as the CARING TRADE of VALUE for VALUE, everyone comes out a winner: the client, the agency, the volunteer program and its director, the donor, the volunteers, and the general public!

In this value exchange, people experience joy as needs are met, and they have the opportunity to feel needed.

In Milton Mayeroff's book *On Caring* he quotes Andras Angyal:

"We ourselves want to be needed. We do not only have needs, we are also strongly motivated by neededness . . . we are restless when we are not needed, because we feel "unfinished," "incomplete" and we can only get completed in and through these relationships. We are motivated to search not only for what we lack and need but also for that which we are needed, what is wanted from us."

Or as Rocky would say:

"We fill each other's gaps."

CHAPTER FIVE — REFERENCES

1. Theodore Levitt, *The Marketing Imagination,* The Free Press, 1983.
2. Philip Kotler, *Marketing for Non-Profit Organizations,* Prentice Hall, 1975.
3. William Cohen and Marshall Reddick, *Successful Marketing for Small Businesses,* Amacom, 1981.
4. Ibid.
5. Ibid.
6. Levitt, *The marketing Imagination.*
7. Alan Schoonmaker, *Selling: The Psychological Approach,* Control Data Education Co., 1978.
8. Ibid.

CHAPTER VI

Getting Your Message Across . . . Advertising, Promotion, Publicity, and Personal Selling

"Everything about an organization talks."
. . . Phillip Kotler[1]

"What you are speaks so loudly I cannot hear what you say."

"Customer relationships are not who you know, but how you are known by them."
. . . Theodore Levitt[2]

As I write this chapter it is the first week of school for students in my home town. Yesterday I was struck by the fact that teachers in our high school, who have not signed a contract for the year as yet, had tapped all four major avenues for getting their message of dissatisfaction across.

In our weekly paper, they had taken out a one-half page ad asking parents not to allow their children to attend school during a teacher's strike . . . that was *advertising*.

In our local newspaper, and on cable TV, information was being offered as to the contract negotiations . . . this was *publicity*.

In front of several key stores in town, the teachers set up card tables, passed out leaflets on the contract problems, and spoke to passersby on the subject . . . this was *promotion*.

123

A "calling chain" has been in effect for some time to keep teachers and key leaders appraised of progress and to keep them aligned and unified . . . this is *personal selling.*

I would be surprised if anyone planning these activities had enough of a marketing background to recognize their four avenues as standard operating procedure for marketing promotion. More likely, they simply used common sense and figured out ways to get their message across to the public.

There's a standard quip that says, "When all else fails, read the directions."

In looking at how to get your message across, or any other aspect of marketing, I offer a paraphrase:

"WHEN ALL ELSE FAILS, USE COMMON SENSE!"

With a few tips and guidelines under your belt, you can devise effective PR campaigns without a year's apprenticeship on Madison Avenue or a $1,000 per day advertising consultant. Let's look at some basic information that will help you design your PR program aspects.

ADVERTISING, PUBLICITY, PROMOTION, PERSONAL SELLING . . .
What's the Difference???

Advertising is a campaign that is designed, pre-tested on target markets, post-tested for results, and presented through selected media in order to influence people to accept a product or idea.

It usually has a theme or slogan and is targeted to specific audiences. It is usually paid for.

Too frequently, groups misunderstand the purpose of advertising, and therefore, they omit testing, targeting, and life-cycle checks, making their ads ineffective.

Phillip Kotler[3] shares: "Advertising is an area of great waste for many organizations. Many . . . fail to clarify the precise objectives they are trying to secure with their advertising, or make the mistake of choosing objectives inappropriate for advertising."

Advertising can serve an organizatioin by making people aware of what they do, what they need, how to contact them, etc. It is usually designed for "quick consumption," not lengthy reading. It is designed to stimulate familiarity.

Tragically, many people confuse advertising with marketing, telling me they have a wonderful "recruitment campaign" going on—24 ads in papers and 100 posters in stores. THIS IS NOT A RECRUITMENT CAMPAIGN—it is an advertising effort that can *augment* recruitment through personalized asking, but by itself is *not* going to be successful in acquiring volunteers, donors, etc.

The most remembered and successful advertising of this century was the "UNCLE SAM WANTS YOU!" campaign that appeared in every post office and train station across the USA during World War II.

Had the posters and ads, however, not been backed up by recruitment offices, appeals, the draft, and the fervor of people wanting to help their country, the ads themselves would have fallen short of their goal.

Publicity "is the development and dissemination of news and promotional material designed to bring favorable attention to a product, person, organization, place, or cause."[4]

It is different from advertising in that it is usually carried by the media free of charge and without indication of the source.

Many groups write stories about clients and find ways to get these stories in newspapers, TV news shows, etc. Others use stories about local volunteers to gain publicity for their group, and still others use events for the same purpose.

Publicity is a creative challenge for your group, as you find ways to use media to tell your story and express needs for support.

It is critical for you to check out the effectiveness of your publicity by finding out how well the public is getting your message. In Chapter II ("What Do You Have") you were challenged to research perceptions of your agency, work, needs, etc. to see if they are aligned with reality.

It is publicity that plays a key role in perceptions and needs to be current, clear, and realistic as it comes across to the public.

Promotion is defined as marketing activities other than personal selling and the two mentioned previously that project your message. Such efforts might include displays, speakers bureau's presentations, booths at local fairs and events, etc. These efforts are usually unique and are not necessarily expected to occur again.

Again, promotions can stimulate the creative minds of your people, as they think of ways to positively gain attention and share information with the public.

Personal Selling: The effective volunteer director understands that some of the best recruiters for their program are satisfied volunteers who relate their positive experiences, and encourage others to become involved. Satisfied donors and supporters can and do play the same role in reaching out to tell your story.

The "catch" in understanding personal selling, however, comes when you separate this promotional activity into its two categories: 1) spontaneous and 2) targeted.

For the most part, the contacts made by donors, volunteers, and supporters is sporadic, unplanned, and happenstance. This is spontaneous personal selling, and it is difficult to measure or control. Most of the people involved in this form of promotion do not even realize what it is; they are simply sharing their pleasure with others.

The second type of personal selling, *targeted,* involves all of the points made in Chapters IV and V. People who are to do the personal selling are chosen carefully, well trained and equipped, motivated, supervised, and evaluated. To secure donors—these are the fundraisers; to obtain volunteers—these are the recruiters; to gain support—these are the advocates or ombudsmen.

These people, whatever their title, zero in on specific individuals or groups who, through research evaluation, are considered prime markets. They design their presentation carefully and follow through for results.

In several of the more marketing-oriented organizations, quotas are even given volunteers and staff, drawing them deeply into profit-organization's technology of sales promotion.

I believe there needs to be effort given to finding middle ground between the volunteer who is unaware that they could recruit support and the person who is given a quota of recruitment calls. That happy medium can come about when volunteers are made aware of the impact they can have on recruitment, offering them tips of how to capture needed information (name, address, position, etc.) for further follow-up and how to seize opportunities to speak on behalf of the organization.

126

HOW FAR THE FOUR METHODS REACH

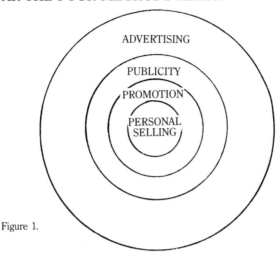

Figure 1.

Figure 1 shows a comparison of all four types of contacts with the size of the circle indicating the number of people that can be reached. This may be helpful in understanding the scope of each method.

Compare this to the four asking techniques described in Chapter V, and you will see that the effectiveness can be ranked in reverse order of numbers of people reached: Most effective: personal selling, (one on one); #2 in effectiveness: promotion (group approach); #3: publicity (phone); #4: advertising (direct mail).

Your decision will need to be made on how you choose to contact people in accordance with the goal of your effort. Do you want many people to know about you or a few, specialized people? Are you simply trying to bring up awareness of opportunities with you, or are you well known and trying to change people's attitudes? Do you need quantity or quality, saturation or specifics, etc.

AN EXERCISE IN PR SELECTION

1. Gather key people from your program; incorporate as many varied perspectives as possible.

2. Explain all four types of promotion.

3. Brainstorm creative ideas in all four categories.

4. Devise plans of action after selecting goals.

FIVE AREAS OF PR FOR VOLUNTEER PROGRAMS

There are five areas of PR that need to be addressed by the volunteer coordinator as they institute an organization-wide marketing climate. These five areas are:[5]

1. *Internal Communications*—Don't overlook the value of marketing your "products" internally. Often when people working with you are kept up to date on events, needs, services, etc. they can refer people and contacts. Keep people "up" on what's going on—WHAT PEOPLE ARE NOT "UP" ON, THEY WILL BE DOWN ON!

2. *External Communications*—Newsletters, annual report, speakers bureau, etc. Newsletters are often overlooked as a "product" and simply given to members of an organizatiion. Begin to see your newsletter as a tool to involve, inform, and recruit people outside or only minimally connected to you: other community groups, past members, suppliers, potential "agents," donors, key leaders in your community, etc. Also consider selling your newsletter to subscribers, if indeed it offers helpful (rather than chatty) information.

3. *Public Relations*—"Activities undertaken by an organization to promote a favorable relationship with the public."[6] The items discussed in the first part of this chapter are facets of PR.

4. *Promotion*—Making your organization the one people want to become involved with. These are your marketing plans projected to the community . . . targeted efforts to tell people what is needed from and offered to them in a value exchange.

5. *Press and Publicity*—Telling your story to the public. (See suggestions that follow.)

PUBLICITY TIPS

When you decide that you will try to use publicity to assist your overall marketing, there are specific tips which may help you get your message across more effectively. Let's look at some of them.

NEWSPAPERS

1. Know who the key reporters/editors are on your local papers and who is assigned to handle your stories.

2. There are usually too few reporters to cover all the stories in an area. You'll have to really fight to get coverage unless a story associated with you is big.

3. Most of your dealings with the papers will be in the form of news releases. Make sure they are:

    a. Clearly, professionally written (remember the five "W's" of journalism—who/when/where/what/how).

    b. Type all copy, double space, and add name, organization, phone number.

    c. Attach photos if possible.

4. Learn the deadlines of all papers.

5. Never give one paper something and not the others if you have multiple papers in town.

6. Make your copy interesting.

7. Make your publicity easy to acquire.

8. If you have an event that can bring you publicity, make sure the reporter knows it's important. Augment releases on speakers, events, etc. with a personal call to add interesting details.

9. Make sure the information is current or in the future. An event last week is not news.

10. Don't assume the reporter/editor/knows your subject as well as you do.

11. Include local involvement if possible.

12. Identify reoccurring advertisers (department stores, realtors, etc.) and ask them to give you some of their space to promote your event, etc.

This work can be done most effectively by a volunteer with a journalism background!

TV/RADIO

1. Look into the opportunities to get your story on the new cable stations that dot the country. They are frequently eager for news that can impact the community.

2. If you have information to share, do so in the early part of the day in case they might want a taped or live interview on their news programs.

3. Know *who* to talk to at the station.

4. Offer yourself or someone else from your agency as an expert resource in your field. Choose carefully—not everyone comes across well on T.V.!

5. Be excited about your publicity. Be creative in presenting it.

6. Tailor publicity so it is seen as beneficial to the community as possible.

7. Consider recruiting the TV or radio stations to participate (and even "co-sponsor") fundraising or promotional events in your community.

8. Provide video tools for TV and audio for radio. The more of a package you can offer the better!

NEWSLETTERS/HOUSE ORGANS OF OTHERS

1. Identify newsletters and company house organs that could be used for publicity purposes.

2. From your resource inventory, identify people with connections to these publications who might get your information into them. Write human interest stories about workers who are volunteering and ask that they be printed.

3. Learn deadlines, editors, space, and content limitations.

4. Develop relationships with editors, find out what they need, and look for something you can trade for their space.

PROMOTION TIPS

Remember that these are usually one time efforts that are unique.

HAND OUTS

1. Identify those stores, utilities, banks, etc. that would be willing to hand out pamphlets and/or place inserts in bills to promote your efforts.

2. Have someone look into any regulations governing handbills etc. put on auto windows, given out on street corners, etc.

IDEAS AND SUGGESTIONS

1. Identify bulletin boards, marques, and billboards that might be available for your use.

2. Consider a speakers bureau to tell your story to groups. Train these people and equip them with visual aids that tell the story of the *clients* served. Remember that every service club in town needs a speaker every week. (Never offer more presentations than you can deliver!)

3. Consider a booth at a local shopping mall or town event (4th of July festival, art show, etc.) that promotes your work, need for volunteers, support, etc.

4. Look at the possibility of tag days or collection drives.

5. Consider fundraising events from the angle of making money and also gaining publicity/recruiting volunteers. Such events might be a-thons (walk/bike/hike/rock, etc.), luncheon or dinners, road rallys, clean-up, theater parties, etc.

6. Consider sale of goods—candy, flags, litter bags, etc. Give information and promotion items along with goods.

7. Enter a float in local parades to publicize your event/program.

8. Grant a scholarship to local youth who give their time to your cause.

9. Sponsor a "poster contest" for school age kids—use posters around the community.

ADVERTISING TIPS

If your budget and energies permit, you can initiate an ad campaign to promote your marketing efforts. Switch to thinking of your offerings as products, and proceed to promote them through your ads.

1. Keep your message simple.

2. Get professional help in designing ads.

3. Get a proofreader to look over your ads.

4. Decide on a theme and stick to it. Use symbolism to project an image.

5. Have ads project client's needs.

6. Give contact information clearly, prominently.

7. Use color when possible, surrounded by good white space.

8. Tell people (in simple words) how effective you are.

9. Show people in your ads.

10. Don't assume your name tells everyone what you do. Research this.

11. Pre and post test ads for effectiveness.

12. Rely on research to see if ads "hit the spot."

13. Target ads carefully!

14. Be creative!

THE "NEEDS" CATALOG

A tool that you might wish to consider which can promote, advertise, and publicize all at one time is a catalog that lists your specific needs.

Subdivide the catalog into "People," "Goods," and "Services" categories so that readers can have many different ways to offer help.

This catalog can also have basic information on what your agency does, who it serves, how it is governed, its financial structure, how volunteers are utilized, history, etc. Contact information is very prominent and "ads" for goods sold by your organization to raise money are displayed.

When this catalog is distributed to targeted markets (past donors, people interested in your cause, clients, churches, service clubs, etc.) it becomes a tool for recruitment, fundraising, and promotion of your organization.

SPEAK PLAIN ENGLISH . . .

Betty Mitchell, dear friend and the pour soul who must decipher my scribblings in order that you can read my books, recently gave me the following, asking me if I could figure out what famous sayings they were:

#1: "One sample of the genus *Malus,* ingested every twenty-four hours, will make superfluous the services of a physician."

and

#2: "Crytogamous concretion never grow on mineral fragments that decline repose."

In case that looks like Greek to You, I assure you it's not! The two famous sayings above are confusing rewrites that make them almost impossible to recognize *or* understand.

Frequently, in marketing, there is a tendency to use complex or fancy working. I suppose some people think that if the words are fancy, people will think the product is too.

Not so.

When messages are unclear they provide a barrier of understanding, give people a really good reason to say "NO," and frankly, disgust people who see through the ploy to "dress" something up.

People respond best when messages are clear, when titles subscribe to the "truth-in-packaging" theory, and when plain language is used.

NEVER USE QUARTER (25 cents) WORDS WHEN NICKLE (5 cents) ONES WILL DO!

Oh, and by the way, the preceding famous sayings, if you haven't figured them out yet are:

#1 "An apple a day keeps the doctor away."

and

#2 "A rolling stone gathers no moss."

MAKING YOUR FINANCIAL PICTURE CLEAR

An extension of clarity in words is the effort I urge you to make in telling people where your money comes from and where it goes. This clarity removes many people's reluctance to become involved, can establish trust ("They must not have anything to hide!"), and encourage participation.

I recommend a pie-chart for income and expenditures to allow people a graphic understanding of your figures. This makes your financial picture clear and easy to read.

HOW TO WRITE A NEWSPAPER ARTICLE

When a newspaper article is written well and sent to the right person on the paper's staff at the right time (deadline) it will have the greatest chance of getting printed.

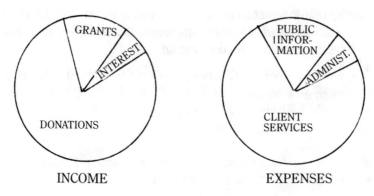

Figure 2.

Specific rules regarding articles can guide your publicity director toward success:

1. Always *type* copy, double spaced.

2. Keep it short, crisp, and to the point.

3. Identify the writer, add phone number, etc.

4. Include the 5 "W's":

    a. Who—use titles correctly; make sure spelling is accurate. Name local people where possible.

    b. When—tell when action occurs; insure news is timely.

    c. What—what's happening? Be specific and clear. State facts, don't editorialize.

    d. Where—give specific information that tells reader where action is to take place.

    e. How—explain specifics of how the action is to come about.

5. Use simple words; avoid jargon; keep sentences and paragraphs short.

6. Understand "inverted pyramid" concept which puts the most important information in the first paragraph, the next most important in the second, and so on. This allows the editor to cut down on the length of your article without cutting important information. (Cuts usually occur for spacing needs.)

7. Use photos when possible; identify people seen in photo; write "cut line copy" (information under photo) for use by paper.

134

8. You can suggest a headline for your article, but don't be shocked if it's not used. Most papers have a "head" writer that specializes in heading creation and spacing.

9. Try to write different stories for different papers. If you need to submit the same information to multiple papers simultaneously, vary the copy.

10. Understand the difference between a news story and a feature story.

   a. News story—relates some action (event, meeting, budget release, etc.) occuring *now*.

   b. Feature—tells a story, is longer, can be in many time frames, has opportunity for emotional appeal.

CONCLUSION

Getting your message across is a vital part of any marketing efforts. Many avenues are open to you, and you must carefully assess which will be most effective for each aspect of your work.

Carefully chosen volunteers with particular skills in communication, journalism, public speaking, broadcasting, etc. can be invaluable in your efforts.

In designing your messages keep the golden rule of communication in mind:

"Keep it simple; make it breathe!"

CHAPTER SIX — REFERENCES

1. Philip Kotler, *Marketing for Nonprofit Organizations,* Prentice Hall, 1975.
2. Theodore Levitt, *The Marketing Imagination,* The Free Press, 1983.
3. Kotler, p. 72.
4. Ibid., p. 73.
5. Joan Flanagan, *The Successful Volunteer Organization,* Contemporary Books, Inc., 1981.
6. Ibid., p. 236.

CHAPTER VII

Marketing Application

"It is not very difficult to persuade people to do
what they are all longing to do."
. . . Aldous Huxley

This book has presented the basic fundamentals of marketing, translating them along the way to circumstances and acceptable terminology of the world of volunteerism.

As each fundamental was introduced, it was explained in order to remove any mystery that might have surrounded it.

As promised in the introduction, I will end this work with step by step guidelines for application of marketing to fundraising, recruitment, and support efforts.

Each step has been explained elsewhere in the book—its rationale, definition, procedure, etc. I have made no attempt to cross reference each step to the pages of its explanation (I will leave that to all you left-brain readers, should you have nothing better to do one winter's evening!)

No step by step checklist of activities can be *exactly* what a reader needs, as there are too many variables for each fundraising, recruitments, and support effort. Generally, however, the steps should guide your path as you work to bring the magic of marketing to your efforts.

Good Luck!

MARKETING AND FUNDRAISING

The principles of marketing are at the core of fundraising, as it creates a value exchange between donor and agency to benefit clients. Fundraising is really "friendraising," and as such cares compassionately about the value returned to the donor.

I. What Do You Have?

    A. What structure is in your organization? How many volunteers? Paid staff?

    B. Is there a total-organization marketing commitment?

    C. Create a large master calendar for your year:

        1. Mark off school, national, and religious holidays.

        2. Secure from the police department or city offices the dates of any competing events.

        3. Secure from key groups in town dates of any fundraising campaigns they are undertaking.

        4. Add the times/dates of high demand internally—report times, board meetings, budget prep time, volunteer events, staff parties, other fundraising efforts, including any United Way campaign times.

    D. Be clear about any restrictions imposed if you are a United Way agency. Understand that more and more United Way agencies are able to do separate fundraising by negotiating this permission with United Way.

    E. Inventory:

        1. Volunteer strengths (skills, experiences, contacts, etc.).

        2. Services you might trade for support from others.

        3. Goods, site-use, etc. you might offer in trade.

        4. Past support:

     a. Groups or businesses who have helped in past

     b. Donors

     c. "Heavy" donors (have given *large* support)

     d. Foundations

     e. Publicity help

     f. Donor profile

D. Check on latest statistics on demographics in your area: ages, median income, employment, population, trends, values, etc.

E. What fundraising efforts (events, campaigns, etc.) have occurred in your community in the last year? How did they do? How were they received?

F. What publics surround you?

    1. Service groups, churches, agencies, competing organizations, schools, health care groups, etc.

    2. Social groups, clubs.

    3. Youth organizations and programs.

    4. Businesses, unions, companies, Chamber of Commerces, etc.

    5. Groups by generic quality: youth, seniors, married, singles, employed, handicapped.

    6. Governing bodies, boards, government, military.

    7. Charities, national associations, VAC's, DOVIA's, etc.

    8. Your own hierarchy.

    9. Internal publics: volunteers, paid staff, board, etc.

   10. People (agents) who speak in your behalf: ministers, VACs, police, welfare departments, etc.

G. What major trends might impact or influence your fundraising effort? Volunteers, megatrends, giving patterns, etc.

H. What perception does the public have of your agency? What is the perception of the fundraising efforts you are considering?

I. What business do you consider yourself to be in? How clear is this to the public?

J. What publicity and promotional avenues are open to you for your fundraising effort?

K. What fundraising efforts are options for your size and strength of agency? Do you have people who could lead these efforts?

L. Do you have the needed potential donors for each option considered above?

M. Do you have an urgent need that can be envisioned by the potential donors?

N. What is the climate of your community? Positive or negative? Hopeful or discouraging?

O. Define what market segments you might target.

P. What makes your services different and unique from others? What might make your fundraising effort unique?

Q. What support groups would you be able to draw on personally as you spearhead your effort?

II. What Do You Need?

A. Identify your goal for fundraising.

B. Using brainstorming ideas generated in Part I regarding fundraising options, which fit your goal most effectively? Decide on the effort (event, campaign, etc.)

C. What organization will you need to carry this effort out?
   1. Leadership
   2. Management chart
   3. Timeline
   4. Workers
   5. Logistics
   6. Budget
   7. Promotional activities
   8. Supplies, physical support
   9. Permits, insurance, etc.

D. Which publics can be targeted markets for you? Which publics can offer you what you need?

E. Have you separated out needs from wants? What people, goods, skills, structure, services, support, and dollars do you *need?* Prioritize needs.

F. How will you recruit workers? Donors? Examine recruitment efforts. Insure concern for fair value trade between donor/volunteer and agency. Avoid unethical recruitment ploys.

G. What attitude is needed to carry this effort? How can you establish a climate to insure this attitude?

III. Who Has What You Need?

A. Zero in, through the evaluation done previously, on those markets you feel would be most likely to have a relationship with you. (Donors, supporters, volunteers, etc.)

B. Do your homework on each market through your resource file.

C. Create a marketing plan for each need, listing:

1. Specific need.
2. Markets that could meet this need.
3. Contacts in each market.
4. What values might your agency offer in trade?
5. Who is the right person to contact them?
6. All possible information on market:

   a. For individuals: motivation, past giving, needs, etc.
   b. For groups: creed, goals, past giving, leadership, fiscal year, meeting times, etc.
   c. For businesses: key people, product or service, past giving, philosophy, financial information, etc.
   d. For foundations: giving patterns and guide lines, key contact, fiscal year, etc.

D. Understand motivations

1. Needs
2. Motivators
3. Theories of satisfaction
4. Expectations

E. Understand people's reason to volunteer. Which categories could your effort meet?

F. Understand people's giving patterns. Which could your event match?

IV. How Do You Get What You Need?

A. What medium will you choose to get your needs met? What fundraising effort: Event? Campaign? Social/fundraising combination? On-going effort? Heavy-donor appeal?

B. For your effort will you choose an undifferentiated, concentrated, or differentiated marketing approach. Decide on one and pursue.

C. After choosing your effort decide:
1. What your "product" is—appeal, features, etc.
2. How you will "price" it—money, time and energy costs, etc.
3. How you will "place" it—how to get to donors, public, etc.
4. How you will "promote" it—ads, promotions, publicity, or personal appeals, etc.

D. What is the life cycle of your effort? Where are you in that cycle? Is there a need to modify your effort? Introduce a new effort? Drop an over-used effort?

E. What satisfactions might your effort provide to participants?

F. Determine methods of asking:
1. One on one—personalized?
2. Group asking—personalized?
3. Phone requests—from friends, from strangers?
4. Mail requests—personalized, shot-gun style?

G. Train people how to ask:
1. Opening
2. Body
3. Diagnosing and removing nos
4. Hidden questions
5. How to close
6. Follow-up
7. Body language
8. Back up material
9. How to relate to different types of people
10. Speaking the prospect's language
11. Ethical statements
12. Never promise what you can't deliver
13. Do your homework

H. Understand dangers in asking.

I. Avoiding specific asking techniques (conning, blaming, negativism, guilt, etc.)

J. Establish your trade relationship with people/groups—getting what you need in exchange for offering what the other party needs.

K. Ask for clients served—not the organization.

MARKETING AND RECRUITMENT

Most top recruiters have not even been aware that they are using the principles of marketing as they enlist people to work in their programs, but that's exactly what they have been doing!

I. What Do You Have?

A. What's the attitude toward recruitment in your agency? Do people think it's your job? The paid staff's? Other volunteers? Or a mixture of all three?

B. What help can your structure lend in recruiting volunteers?

C. What present volunteers belong to other groups that might provide recruits? Identify each along with information on meeting times, leadership, and how to best approach them as a group.

D. Create a master calendar of your organization's demands. Add school, church, and national holidays. Research and add competing demands from groups you might be contacting. From this, select options for best timing for recruitment.

E. What types of recruitment have you done in the past? What were the results? When did these efforts occur?

F. What are the general trends surrounding your organization? Demographics of working people, age, finances, employment, etc.

G. Identify reasons people might want to work with you—your tangible and intangible benefits.

H. Look over your inventory of goods, services, people, status, etc. you might offer in a trade relationship to volunteers.

I. What publics surround you? With which have you had relationships in the past?

J. Which groups that surround you have like goals on values with your agency? Who are the key leaders in each? What contacts do you have with them?

K. What perception does the public have of your agency and its work? Its clients? Effectiveness? Volunteers?

L. What business do you consider yourself in as an agency? As a volunteer program?

M. What support would you personally have as you undertake a recruitment effort?

N. What options are available for recruitment: campaign, one major effort, informal, formal?

O. What promotional and publicity avenues and medium are open to you? Who are the key contacts within those avenues?

P. What potential volunteer members are available in your area?

Q. Define which market segments you might target.

R. What makes your agency/program different from others?

II. What Do You Need?

A. Why do you need volunteers? What would they do?

B. What goals would be met if volunteers were recruited?

C. What are your recruitment goals?

D. What specifically do you need?
   1. Numbers of people
   2. Specific skills and/or experience
   3. Job designs
   4. Plans of action
   5. Organization (management) of recruitment efforts
   6. Organization (management) of work to be done by recruits.
   7. Materials and supplies needed for recruitment and work

E. Which publics can be targeted for recruitment efforts?

F. Have you separated needs from wants in terms of recruits?

G. What methods will be used to recruit? How will you insure avoiding negative recruitment tactics?

H. What attitude will be needed to successfully complete your recruitment efforts? What attitude exists now?

I. Do your present volunteers see themselves as recruiters? How can you capitalize on this?

III. Who Has What You Need?

    A. Identify most likely markets to give you who you need based on information and screening done in part II.

    B. Research information on each market above through your resource file.

    C. Prioritize markets based on research, choosing those that seem most likely to be open to a relationship and with whom you have the most contacts.

    D. Create a marketing chart that shows your specific needs for volunteers, the available markets who might provide your recruits, contact people, what you might offer in trade of values, specific data on each market.

    E. When planning to recruit individually, know:

        1. Past involvement
        2. Special skills, talents, likes
        3. Motivation
        4. Availability

    F. When planning to recruit a group, know:

        1. Who to talk to to secure permission to speak.
        2. Logistics of meeting site, time, agenda, etc.
        3. Their creed/slogans in order to use words in request.
        4. How they receive recognition as a group; can you provide a way for them to get this?
        5. What their past history is with your group and others.
        6. Who are key leaders.
        7. Who might support/oppose you in the group and why.

    G. Understand motivations of people and groups.

    H. Understand people's reasons for volunteering.

IV. How Do You Get What You need?

    A. What is the best way for you to recruit the people you need?

    B. Will your approach be differentiated, undifferentiated or concentrated? Choose and proceed.

    C. Your volunteer jobs are your "product." What features, appeal will it have?

    D. How will you "price" your product—time, costs, energy?

E. How will you make your recruitment effort available to the public? How will you make contact with potential donors?

F. How will you promote your efforts? Ads, publicity, speakers bureaus?

G. How "new" is the work you offer? How flexible is it? How much does it dovetail with the needs of modern volunteers?

H. What opportunities for flexibility exist in your product?

I. Who will do the asking in recruitment?

J. How will you prepare your recruiters so they know how to ask—What training will be provided?

K. What satisfactions might you offer prospective volunteers?

L. How will recruiters be trained to know:
    1. How to deal with different kinds of people.
    2. Diagnose and remove objections.
    3. Understand and be prepared for hidden questions.
    4. Find out about the recruits needs, gifts, motivations, personal demands of family, work, etc.
    5. Body language.
    6. Importance of congruity and how to listen.
    7. How to remain ethical.
    8. How to be flexible in job assignments, matching right people to right jobs.
    9. How to be even more concerned with the needs of the recruits than simply "fill a slot."
    10. Never to promise what can't be delivered.
    11. To always do their homework.
    12. How to speak the language of the recruit.

M. Insure recruiters avoid dangers in asking, and reject unfair asking techniques.

N. Insure recruiters ask in the name of the clients that can be served.

O. Be clear and concise on what the volunteer is needed for, what benefits they will get, how long they will do the work, etc.

P. Choose best timing for efforts and organize carefully.

Q. Create awareness in present volunteers of need for their help. Provide them with a simple way to record name, phone number, etc. of anyone showing interest in their work.

MARKETING TO GAIN SUPPORT

There will be many times during your work when you will need to secure support from individuals, groups or the general public.

Your needs will vary, and in their variances, will cause you to strategize differently. At one point you may need the support of your boss in introducing a new program aspect in your volunteer department; at another time you may need the support of the board of directors as you seek to serve a newly identified client need; at still another you may need the support of the public in bringing about a change in your community.

Again, however, with modification tailored to each need for support, the principles of marketing are your magic tool for success.

I. What Do You Have?

    A. You will have to have a clear and honest appraisal of the structure that now makes up your organization:

        1. Who are the key people?

        2. Who has the power to make things happen?

        3. What people, inside your organization, are aligned with one another? Against one another?

        4. What major issues are these people dealing with at the present? What demands are placed on them?

        5. Has your issue been before the power structure before? What happened?

        6. What "political" issues are going to be touched if you proceed in your quest for support?

    B. A clear and honest appraisal of support that might surround you:

        1. Are there any groups that already have in place what you are needing? How successful are they working? What are documented results of this other-agency's efforts?

2. What people, connected to you, have contacts with other groups who have implemented your request?

C. What trends and demographics surround you that would strengthen your appeal and justification for the action you are requesting?

D. What makes your request different from others?

E. What attitude or climate exists in your agency now? How positive is it? How receptive will workers be if your request is granted?

F. What is the procedure for decision making in your group? Formal? Informal? Much paperwork? A handshake?

II. What Do You Need?

A. What specifically do you need? Authority, budget, workers, permission to continue, promotion, etc.

B. What process would you need if permission is granted?

C. What time would you need to pursue your request? What would it cost in dollars?

D. What numbers of people would be needed to carry out your proposal? What special skills would be needed? Who would supervise these people? When? How?

E. What promotional tools (graphs, slide shows, endorsements, etc.) would be needed to explain your proposal, etc.?

F. What attitude or climate would be necessary before the effort could be a success?

III. Who Has What You Need?

A. Looking at identified power sources in and out of your agency (these are "publics" also), which would be able to grant your needs? Which would be able to help persuade the power sources to grant your needs?

B. Create a marketing chart for each need (prioritized) listing:

1. Specific need.

2. Who might be able to meet that need (a targeted market).

3. Who has contacts to each market.

4. What information can be gathered for each market?

5. Who is the best person to contact them.

6. What offers in trade can be made to each market in exchange for their support?

C. Understand motivation theories well.

D. What kind of marketing will you use: differentiated, concentrated, undifferentiated? Decide and pursue.

IV. How Do You Get What You Need?

A. Strategize approach—differentiated, undifferentiated or concentrated.

B. Make all appeals for support *in person*.

C. Understand art of asking:

1. Speak language of power source.

2. List benefits.

3. Diagnose and remove objections.

4. Understand ways people relate.

D. Design approach to each power source carefully. Know what turns them on, turns them off.

E. Respect their position.

F. Ask for clients helped.

G. Persuade—don't dictate.

H. Be flexible—a "one-way" approach is bad.

I. Avoid "con-games." Be ethical at all times!

J. Secure the authority you need *in writing*.

CONCLUSION

If you are still with me at this last point on the book, I can only assume:

1. You liked it, or. . . .

2. You are a glutten for punishment, or . . .

3. You are snowed in, the T. V. is broken and you could find nothing else to read, or. . . .

4. You are a graduate of the Indianapolis Home for the Silly!

If you have read it in one sitting, I'll know that probably #s 2, 3, & 4 are *all* applicable and simply extend my sympathies!

Actually, I will hope that in reading this work, you found several "ah-has", a few "wows!" and even a "tee-hee" or two.

My fondest hope, however, is that you now feel comfortable with the incredibly valuable tool of MARKETING, understanding the magic it can bring to your program and the miracles it can create in your quest to serve more people effectively.

History has been blessed with caring people who have voluntarily taken on responsibilities that help others. In return they have received the priceless rewards of feeling needed, helpful, enhanced and effective. Without knowing it they have employed the best principles of marketing . . . the caring trade of value for value.

When we, as directors of programs that seek to serve others through this voluntary spirit, understand more clearly the tool of marketing, we will enable even more people to be touched by it's magic . . . the magic of making dreams come true.

. . . . Sue Vineyard

151